O_h M_y G_{osh}!

......IT'S ALL REAL!

O_h M_y G_{osh}!
......IT'S ALL REAL!

From Atheist

to Religion and

Finally—the Truth

A True Story of Supernatural Encounters

SIMON BETHEL

Copyright © 2017 Simon Bethel.

All rights reserved. No part of this book may be used or reproduced by any means, graphic, electronic, or mechanical, including photocopying, recording, taping or by any information storage retrieval system without the written permission of the author except in the case of brief quotations embodied in critical articles and reviews.

Because of the dynamic nature of the Internet, any web addresses or links contained in this book may have changed since publication and may no longer be valid. The views expressed in this work are solely those of the author and do not necessarily reflect the views of the publisher, and the publisher hereby disclaims any responsibility for them.

This book is a work of non-fiction. Unless otherwise noted, the author and the publisher make no explicit guarantees as to the accuracy of the information contained in this book and in some cases, names of people and places have been altered to protect their privacy.

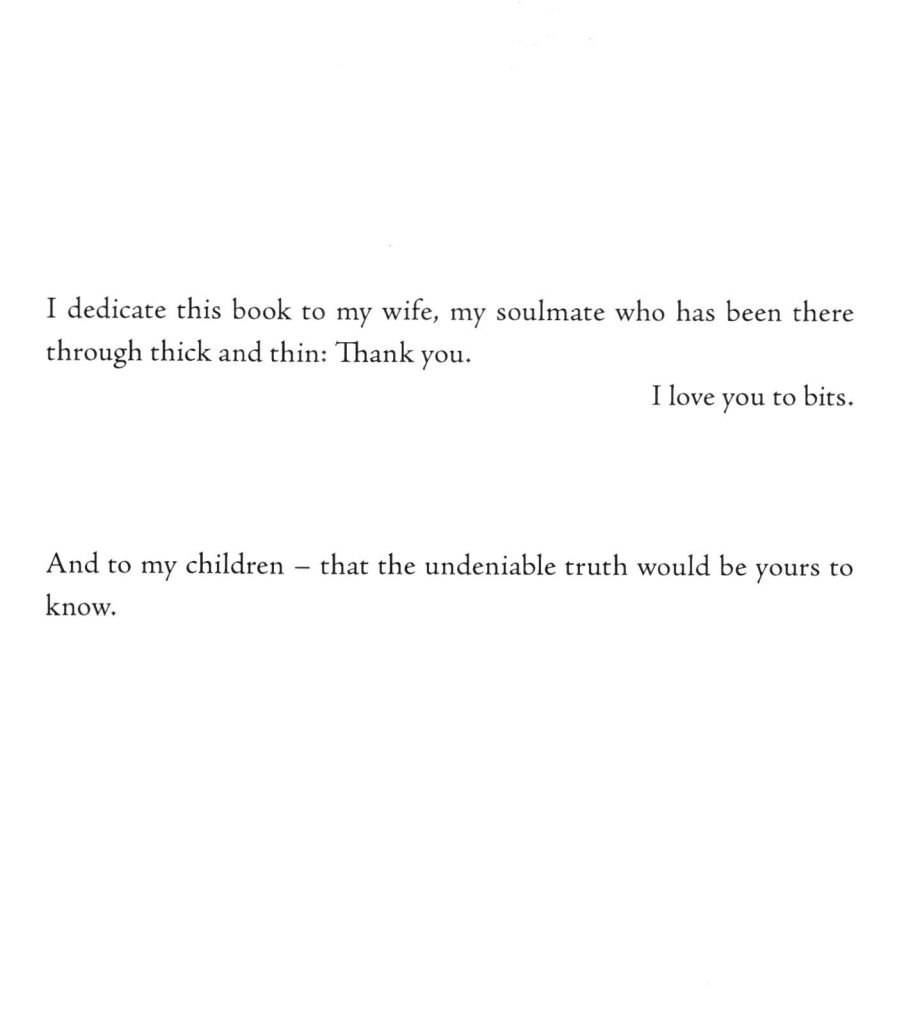

I dedicate this book to my wife, my soulmate who has been there through thick and thin: Thank you.

> I love you to bits.

And to my children – that the undeniable truth would be yours to know.

CONTENTS

Foreword ix
Prologue xiii

Part 1. My Early Years

CHAPTER 1   The Early Years: A Lot of Pain 3
CHAPTER 2   A Challenge, a Very Bumpy Road, and an Encounter 23
CHAPTER 3   The Storm Gets Darker, but There Is a Light in the Clouds 32

Part 2. I Get Religion

CHAPTER 4   An Angel Arrives, and God Intervenes 43
CHAPTER 5   A Very Rocky Road, but God Is Right in the Middle of It 54
CHAPTER 6   Time for a Change and to Turn up the Light .. 68

Part 3. The Truth at Last

CHAPTER 7	My Train Crashes off the Rails, but God Makes His Big Move	75
CHAPTER 8	Clear out Your Baggage: Time for a Crazy Life with God	85
CHAPTER 9	What Could Possibly Happen Next?	96
CHAPTER 10	Hang on Tight and Ride that Bull; God Is on It with You Too	110
CHAPTER 11	Things Just Get Crazier, but It appears to be God's Normal	130
CHAPTER 12	An even crazier natural but still normal for the Lord	144
CHAPTER 13	Worship? Really?	157
CHAPTER 14	Conclusion	168

FOREWORD

One of my heroes is John Wesley. And there are two small accounts from his journals that help me sum up my knowledge of Simon – who you are about to get to know through the pages of this book.

The first scene is when John Wesley – fully ordained and preaching the gospel – had set foot on American soil to be a missionary to the natives. He had gone with the Moravians. But he had obviously gone on mission in his own strength. On Saturday, 7 February 1736, Mr Wesley has a conversation with a Mr Sprangenberg, a German pastor of the Moravians.

He said to Wesley, "My brother, I must first of all ask you one or two questions. Have you the witness within yourself? Does the Spirit of God bear witness with your spirit, that you are a child of God?"

Wesley tried to give a reasoned answer based on his own knowledge from being a Bible scholar: "I know he is the Saviour of the World."

"True," he replied, "but do you know he has saved you?"

Wesley answered, "I hope he died to save me."

His questioner only added, "Do you know yourself?"

Wesley said, "I do," but in his journal, he went on to say, "I fear they were vain words."

When I first met Simon, he came across as a highly successful businessman with a very good looking family. He was an enthusiastic supporter of my ministry in his local church. But he never was totally committed. He often said that he could see the path of faith he should be on, but he was on the outside looking in. I would later find out that there had been things in his life that stopped him from walking that path. Simon's faith was very much powered by his knowledge, quick thinking, and smooth talk. It was very much talking the talk but not walking the walk.

Going back to my hero, Mr Wesley, it was two years later in London that his experience of God and his ministry ignited into the great man of revival he became. On 14 May 1738, he wrote, "In the evening I went very unwillingly to a society in Aldersgate street where one was reading Luther's Epistle to the Romans. About a quarter before nine, while he was describing the change which God works in the hearts through faith in Christ, I felt my heart strangely warmed. I felt I did trust in Christ, Christ alone for salvation: and an assurance was given me that he had taken away my sins, even mine, and saved me from the law of sin and death."

This was a paradigm shift of Holy Spirit proportions which would ignite a ministry and see thousands come to Christ.

I won't spoil Simon's story, but all I can say is that I witnessed his "heart strangely warmed" moment. I can testify that since this happened and since I found him on his knees repenting in my study, Simon's life has changed. His passion for Jesus has blown me away. I have ended up doing crazy things with him like treasure-hunting prayer walks and praying in a church at 3 a.m. and laughing in the spirit so much that my sides felt like splitting.

The true story that Simon is about to tell you is of a normal bloke, a successful businessman, a family man. Not a trained clergyman but a man with a passion for Jesus who really does believe that faith the size of a mustard seed can move mountains.

I commend this book to you and hope that it will inspire your faith and passion for Jesus. If you don't yet know Jesus, well, read on because you will find out how a normal bloke from the north of England found out Jesus was real, fell in love with him, and wants to serve him for the rest of his days.

Reverend Wesley Rocca
Methodist minister

PROLOGUE

I have often chatted with people about various events in my journey through life, and each time I have, they said something like, "That is amazing; you should write a book about it."

My response has always been, "You should hear the full story; now that is book and a half!"

Having had this conversation numerous times, I thought that actually, my life has been an amazing one. No one has heard my full story, and so I thought it was time for me to write it down so that I could share it properly.

This book represents a brief summary of my life so far and charts life's twists and turns as a normal person goes through adversity and success; it's a powerful spiritual journey that has taken some surprising turns. Everything I have written in these pages is true and represents my journey from atheism to religion and finally arriving at the truth, the latter being revealed through some powerful supernatural encounters.

The stories have been read by those involved, who have confirmed that I have retold accounts of what happened accurately and that the words on the page represent a true account of events.

I offer this book as a living testimony to the truth, a truth that has taken me by surprise and changed my life forever. I hope you will find the truth as you read on.

PART 1.

MY EARLY YEARS

CHAPTER 1

The Early Years: A Lot of Pain

It was five thirty in the morning on a wet and windy autumn morning in October 1967, and a young woman had just been admitted to a hospital, in labour with her first child. As the wind and rain thrashed around outside, inside she was having her own storm as she wrestled though her labour in the sparse delivery room. Without any sedation or pain relief, she fought for two hours until her son was finally brought into the world. As the newborn took his first breath, the doctor made a close inspection of the fine specimen of a boy to make sure that all was well. As he scanned and checked the little one, he noticed something was not right. What was that noise he could hear? It was the sound of running water; was there a leak? No, it was the sound of the baby urinating down the front of the doctor's clean white coat. It was okay; everything was working. I had made my entrance.

I had been born into modest surroundings in a town in the north of England. This was a hard and unforgiving town that had been shaped by the tough environment created from its background of manual labour and hardship. There had been a number of coal mines and steel mills that were full of workers who were hardened to a life of heavy manual labour. Along with neighbouring cities, the town had been a key industrial part of the country. However, from the 1980s onwards, the area had been in decline as the mines and steel mills had slowly been closing. This brought about new difficulties to the townsfolk as people tried to find ways to earn a living. The sum of all this hardship resulted in a town that consisted of hardened, close-knit communities, each one revolving around their own particular industry. These were tough communities that had been forged on an anvil of adversity.

This was the town that I had been born into, and it was a place where I would learn a resilience, grittiness, and tenacity that would serve me well in the coming years. These lessons would develop into some of my core character traits, and over time, stubbornness and selfishness would be added as a result of the difficulties and adversity that I experienced in my own life. These traits would steer me in and out of many difficult circumstances over the coming years.

In some ways, I was fortunate in my upbringing because my parents, who had experienced hardship in their own childhood, were keen to improve their living standards and wanted to raise their family in more comfortable surroundings. They didn't want their children to have to face the same challenges that they had experienced as they grew up. It was a difficult starting point because they had very little. My parents married very young, and our first home was a one-bedroom ground-floor flat in a very modest terraced house quite near to the center of town. It had to be near the center of town because initially there was no car, and so walking or public transport were the means of getting around. It was here that I lived the first few years of my life.

The house itself was an old building, and unfortunately, because of its age, it was quite damp. There was damp in the bedroom, which my parents could never get rid of despite trying lots of different solutions. Over a period of time, this damp atmosphere started to have a detrimental effect on my health. Increasingly, I started to have various bronchial issues and was struggling to breathe properly, all caused by the damp atmosphere. When I was three years old, I became seriously ill with a bad chest infection. The doctor prescribed me with penicillin to help clear the infection, but soon after, I quickly started to deteriorate to a dangerous level.

As my condition worsened, it became evident that I was allergic to the penicillin, and so the doctors took me off the medication. I would get a lot worse before getting any better. I vaguely remember being bedridden and feeling really ill, with my mum looking after me twenty-four hours a day. There was a serious concern over my condition, and various family members came to visit me. It took a while, but fortunately, in the end, I came through this period of ill health, much to the relief of my parents.

I think it was this episode of illness that prompted Mum and Dad to move. They had already been thinking about moving because we only had one bedroom to share in the flat and things were getting a little cramped. But this bout of illness had helped add a sense of urgency to the matter. So after a flurry of activity, it wasn't long before they bought a newer house in a more affluent part of town. At the age of four, I was packed up with all our belongings and moved across town to our new home for a new start……. and with not a single patch of damp in sight!

As the years rolled on and I grew older, I was acutely aware that the town I was growing up in was hard-hearted. It wasn't difficult to go out and hear angry words or vicious arguments between people, and there were places you just didn't feel safe walking through. The environment at home was also filled with harsh words and arguments. It seemed my parents were having relationship difficulties that were spilling emotion out into the house. I started to feel like I needed to escape and get away from the depressing tensions around me. Rather than expose myself to the tough environments inside and outside of home, I opted to find activities that would keep me in much more comfortable surroundings.

In my younger years, I would often be found withdrawing to be alone in my room, playing with my train set or out with the Boy Scouts, camping in different parts of the country. Boy Scouts was a regular weekly event, and it was something that I really enjoyed. Being a practical person, I took pleasure in learning some useful skills for life, such as survival and cooking while at the same time, having fun playing games in a stress free environment. It was also somewhere that I felt like I belonged and the security that came from being in a familiar and stable group was only disrupted by the occasional change of individuals moving in or out of the troop. The group of boys and leaders pretty much remained the same, and therefore it felt like a safe and familiar environment for me to be in where there was no arguing.

At this stage in my life, I was blissfully unaware of my own growing insecurity and fear. This drove my need to find somewhere I felt I was accepted by other people and feel like I had a place in a group among others. I was always comfortable with the familiarity of a regular group. However, put me in a new environment with people I didn't know, and I would become withdrawn and nervous because of my lack of self-confidence. Not only did the Boy Scouts teach me new skills, it provided me a safe place to belong and feel accepted by others.

OH MY GOSH! .....IT'S ALL REAL!

On the flip side of my desire to be accepted and to belong, I also needed somewhere to withdraw, somewhere I could escape to and not have to engage with people I didn't know. My train layout, which was permanently set up in my room, was the perfect escape. I would spend hours alone in my room, building a world into which I could disappear. I was the director of the railway, in charge of the timetable and services. In my mind, I imagined the trains being boarded by commuters, holiday makers, and school parties, and as they travelled through the scenery of trees and hills, I would be lost in a world without cares. Here was a place where I could be confident and strong, and do what I liked without any complications. My train set was my place of hiding and escape, a place where there was no anxiety or stress, a place where there was no one to judge me.

During the seventies and eighties, there was a real sense of fear in the air as the Cold War continued on between Russia and America. It was not uncommon to switch on the television and see a program about nuclear war and how to survive. Some of the programs were graphic, with all the horrors of war, and they stoked up a lot of anxiety in people. It was at this time that I grew through my teenage years, and my own insecurity and lack of self-confidence snowballed. This didn't help me face the many new experiences that were being thrust upon me. I was having to meet new friends in new schools and my parents expected me to perform well in lessons and exams; all this extra pressure stirred up an increasing anxiety within me.

As time went by and I grew older, I needed to progress to more mature activities where I could continue to hide from my anxieties. The train set was replaced by photography which allowed me to continue to spend time alone and build a new imaginary world. I found that a darkroom represented the perfect place where I could shut myself away. I set up a darkroom in our attic so that I could spend even more time creating an imaginary world from behind a camera. This became a place for me to depict a different world on paper where I could spend a lot of time alone, away from the turmoil of the world, viewing it from behind a lens. I continued to need to escape to somewhere I could feel safe and secure.

The Boy Scouts was also replaced by playing in a rugby team. Again, this represented a group to which I could belong. Just like the leaders in the Boy Scouts, there were numerous people to tell me what to do: The coach, the captain, in fact most other team members would tell me what to do. My lack of confidence meant that I needed people to direct me with instruction. I wasn't decisive and needed to be led and guided by others. However, there was an added surprise: Rugby brought something new into the mix; aggression. Living in the volatile environment at home had resulted in me becoming increasingly angry and resentful at the world around me. Combined with living in a tough northern town, I felt like everyone was judgmental and hard-hearted. I found that the aggressive and physical nature of rugby allowed me to vent my frustration and anger. The adrenalin would rise with my anger when I ran at people with the ball, trying to knock them over, or grabbing players to tackle them, or even in the general carnage of a scrum. I could feel a real anger in me and enjoyed letting it out on the rugby field. It was really satisfying hurting others on the field, and whenever I got hurt, I felt like I deserved it. What a mixed-up mess I was; rugby was a great release for my emotions, and I had a lot of them.

If you take the fact that I was a teenage boy going through puberty and mix it up with the emotions generated by all the emerging problems at home, then I represented a real mess. The problem was that you wouldn't have noticed it because I was burying it all deep within me, hidden from prying eyes. I was like a train that was starting to come off the rails. To the outside observer, it all looked like a healthy childhood: I had hobbies and interests, I eagerly played sport, and my behaviour was generally good, whilst academically, I was achieving an average set of results. I am sure that anyone writing about my upbringing would probably say it was similar to a lot of other boys of that time and made for an uneventful childhood, especially with regard to money and the security of a roof over my head….. but inside it was a different story.

This was driven by other aspects of my upbringing would prove to be much more eventful.

My father was a professional footballer. Unfortunately for us, this was in the days before the Internet and the lucrative sports industry of today, with its big wages and sponsorship deals. In those days, it was rare for sport to provide a route to financial success and celebrity status. Nevertheless, my father was well known through the town and being the son of someone well known had its advantages. If I was buying anything such as sports equipment or a car, then my father always had a contact who could get me a great deal. When in local shops or restaurants, I just needed to tell them that he was my dad, and it would usually result in some sort of discount.

This was all great and beneficial to me, but as the years progressed, I started resenting this identity of being continually referred to as "So-and-So's son" and always being directed to do things in a certain way to get a deal by using my father's name. This resentment grew over the years as I felt that it was denying me of my own individuality. I became increasingly insecure in my own ability and, for some reason, increasingly angry about it.

These emotions continued to get worse, and as time passed by, I grew less confident around people. Even though I resented it, I found that my father was always someone for me to hide behind (figuratively speaking) so that I could take the focus of others away from me and my own insecurities.

During the 1970s, my father left his sporting career and moved into a successful business. However, after a few years of this, he missed the enjoyment football gave him and so, on top of working his business during the day, he embarked on building his non-professional sporting activities in the evenings. This meant that he spent increasing amounts of time out of the house. He was becoming less of a feature in my daily life, spending little time with me. In the small amount of time that we did spend together, he would usually complain that he was tired and that I needed to do more round the house to help out at home. When I did help, my efforts would be met with the disappointment of being told that I hadn't done things correctly and I should put more thought and effort into it. I was starting to feel angry, bitter, and emotionally strangled.

I felt like I was being rejected, not appreciated, and it hurt. These emotions were reinforced by memories from my early years of being left behind as a child. When I was young, I would often be left with my grandparents for the weekend, while sport and social events dominated my parents' time. There were many occasions when I would be dropped off on a Saturday for my grandparents and uncles to look after me. I was then collected either late on a Saturday night or some time on Sunday. If it was late on Saturday, I would be scooped up while asleep and be dropped into my parents' car to be taken home at the end of an evening. Otherwise, I was left overnight and collected at some point on Sunday.

My parents obviously had a demanding social life, which resulted in me not seeing them some weekends and on others, going to sleep in one place and waking up back in my own bed. This had happened from a young age and these past memories were now adding to my hurt of feeling rejected.

As well as the rejection, I also had fond memories from those early years. My grandparents had doted on me whenever I stayed at their house, maybe too much because they allowed me to eat as much of whatever I wanted, which added an unhealthy amount of weight to my body…. talk about comfort eating! My grandparents had two of their sons living at home with them (my uncles). They never left and spent most of their lives living at that house, resulting in a very close family. Sometimes when I spent the weekend with them, I would be treated to something special. One uncle took me out to the shops and bought me a toy to play with. My other uncle would take me out on Sunday to walk in the forests and parks in Nottinghamshire. They each had their own ways to spoil me, and over time, I forged some very strong relationships with them.

I always felt welcome in that house and doted on as a grandson and nephew. They seemed to cultivate a welcoming and safe environment for me, in which I felt very comfortable. It was a stark contrast to what I would experience elsewhere as I grew older. Over the coming years, theirs would often be a safe haven for me where I could come and forget all the difficulties that were going on in my life. On a couple of occasions, I pretended to run away and leave home but was easily found because I was too predictable in going to my grandparents' house.

This environment was worlds away from the one at home, where it seemed everything I had done in my life had not been good enough. I remember how when I was very young, I had attempted to learn to play the guitar. I had found it very difficult, and whenever I practiced at home, any encouragement would quickly turn to shouting because I couldn't do it and the sound I produced was awful. This constant negative emotion really affected my spirit, and I was becoming withdrawn, shy, and wary of entering unfamiliar situations. I felt that nothing I tried to do in life met what was expected of me because I had been constantly told that I couldn't do anything right.

All this impacted me in two ways: Firstly, it shook my confidence lower, and secondly, it taught me that everyone I met was constantly judging me. This brought about a growing fear and anxiety of what people thought of me and affected the way I did things and the way I engaged with people. The fear of reproach and being judged resulted in my hesitancy to do anything or make decisions, and I became withdrawn when dealing with others. I was quite nervous and found any new or unfamiliar situations a very painful experience.

However, when I was fifteen years old, I discovered something that could help numb the pain and make me more carefree: alcohol. It became my medicine and helped with the fear and anxiety. What started off as the odd little tipple (stealing a few mouthfuls from a bottle in the drinks cupboard and replacing it with water) progressively picked up the pace, and by the time I was sixteen, I was developing a real taste for drinking alcohol. I even went to school drunk on a few occasions. I would think nothing of having a little tipple prior to an exam to help me loosen up. The acute anxiety in me meant that I needed to drink frequently to numb the pain; this was developing into an addiction.

At the age of fifteen, I found it was easy to drink alcohol unnoticed because an added distraction had arrived in the house….. a new baby. For my first fourteen years, I was the only child and had the sole attention of my parents, which had its ups and downs. In some respects, I was spoiled; I was allowed to go for annual skiing trips with school, got nice Christmas and birthday presents, and even got a puppy for company. However, there was a flip side…. Being the only child meant that I witnessed alone the arguments and constant emotional roller coaster between my parents. I had no one to share the experience with and no one to talk to about what was happening. When an argument erupted, I would try to intervene and diffuse the situation. I learned that by just being in the midst of the tension introduced a distraction that sometimes helped the situation. However, afterwards, I would lay in my bedroom, worrying and feel very alone. I had no one who could listen to me and understand; it was very lonely indeed.

Then, one summer, I went on a week-long scout camp in the south of England with the Boy Scouts. My parents realised they were going to miss me and therefore took a holiday not too far from where we were camping. Even though I was still physically close by, they missed having their child around. I imagine that my first week away from home was a bit of a shock to them and as I became more active and grew older, they noticed that they were spending more time in the house together without me, which was leaving a hole in the family; it was time for a brother or sister for Simon.

When my brother arrived, it changed my world in both good and bad ways. I was no longer the only child, getting all the parental attention. My brother needed more and more of their time, and I started to feel like I was in second place. I am sure that my parents did not mean for me to feel that way, but for me, I really felt this shift of attention away from me to the newborn child. There were times I wanted to talk or do something, but I was dismissed away because my brother needed feeding or rocking to sleep. Due to my complex emotional state, this felt like another layer of rejection had been laid on top of my feelings of not being wanted. This response from my parents added to the anger and resentment already fermenting inside me; it would continue to grow, fuelled by the increasing arguments between my parents.

Despite feeling like this, from the moment he arrived in the family, I was in love with my little brother. I would spend many hours pushing him round the back garden in a pram to get him to go to sleep. As he started to grow through the first few years of his life, we forged a strong brotherly bond. We would play together and, despite the age gap, seemed to grow closer together. I remember my mum commenting on numerous occasions that I was a really good brother and despite the age gap, we were surprisingly close to each other. She would often say, "Not many fourteen-year-old boys would spend the time with their baby brother like Simon does."

As my brother approached four years old, things changed even further. After being the only child for fourteen years and then developing a great relationship with my brother, a little sister now appeared on the scene who was very loud and certainly made her presence known. I would often be woken up in the early hours of the morning by her shouting and screaming just outside my door; suddenly, the house had started to feel crowded. I had finished school and was in college doing my 'A' levels. I was finding my feet outside of the house and I now felt that home was becoming claustrophobic in more ways than one: Physically, there were more people in the house and I had moved into the smallest bedroom so that my brother and sister could share the large bedroom I had occupied for all those years. This was a big culture shock to me, as the new room was a quarter of the size of my previous room. Also, emotionally, the atmosphere at home was not healthy. There were a lot of arguments and disagreements, and I always felt like I was walking on eggshells.

I was still spending time in the darkroom and still playing rugby but was now finding every reason possible to get out of the house. One of the ways to get out was to go to the bars and drink. My new social life was starting to develop. It felt like an escape, and I thoroughly enjoyed it.

It was 1986, and I had passed my driving test, started my first job, and bought my first car, which allowed me to spend even more time out of the house. The job provided money, a key enabler for my independence: money in my pocket to pay for fuel and socialising. As well as the money, I was making a new set of friends who had a very active, fun and appealing social life, and this was opening up a whole new world of sin to me. Over the years, I had received a sheltered upbringing, and I had been shy and reserved for all that time. Now, I was being encouraged to get into things that I had never really experienced before. I was ill prepared for the big wide world and was quickly consumed by the drunken night life it offered. This social life had also provided me with steady girlfriend with whom I was spending an increasing amount of time with. She represented another opportunity to get out of the house and away from the claustrophobia.

All of this time out of the house resulted in me spending an increasing amount of time in bars and clubs. I was developing a greater love (addiction) for alcohol and was now drinking a lot more than was physically good for me. On a night out during the week, I would think nothing of drinking six or seven pints of beer, followed by numerous spirits and at the weekends, I would consume even more. This behaviour resulted in more arguments at home, and I was starting to feel very unhappy; it was time to do something about it. The thought of taking any kind of action scared me, but I was now at my wits' end and couldn't take any more. However, before we move onto that, let's pause for a moment and dig a little deeper into each of these areas of my life that were dragging me into destruction.

Throughout my childhood, my parents had always protected me from a lot of the harsher realities of a cruel world; it would be fair to say that I was very naïve. I grew up with a lack of confidence, weak social skills, and a feeling of being inadequate. In every situation in my life, I would always review what was happening with a self-critical tone, and I was consumed with what other people would think of me. This was borne out of all the criticism I had received throughout the years, being told what I was and wasn't capable of doing and being shouted at when I fell short of expectation. I had repeatedly been told about my limitations and that I would never amount to anything. Having heard this enough times, I had started to believe it was true. I felt that I was unworthy and that I rarely did anything right.

I had accepted these thoughts to be true, which resulted in me always being afraid when doing anything new in my life such as a job interview, meeting people, or entering an unfamiliar situation. I recall that every time I met anyone, my first thoughts were always, *'I wonder what they think of me. When will they notice that I am no good at anything?'* In my mixed-up negative emotion, I was unclear of who I was and who I was becoming.

This uncertainty of who I was had been forged by constantly being referred to as "So-and-So's son." My close friends saw me for who I was, but outside of this circle, my identity as an individual was lost in favour of being known as *someone's* son. I grew increasingly angry at being seen like this and the fact that no one saw Simon for who he really was, but then who was I? I was unsure myself of who I was and what my character was made up of. My resentment about this identity of being seen as *'So and So's son,* which I couldn't seem to shake off, continued to grow, as did my anger.

I am sure there are many people out there who grew up and had people telling them they would never amount to anything, they were no good, or they needed other people to help them get through in life. I am sure that I am not the first or the last person to be told these lies and to have had their confidence knocked down. Many people who have been through such experiences are usually a bottled-up, emotional time bomb waiting to go off. I certainly was.

So when I got into my first serious relationship, I was a bit of an emotional mess. Most of the time, because of my lack of confidence, I was easy to influence and control, but periodically, I would be overwhelmed by these feelings, which would result in an emotional explosion. These explosions took the form of angry outbursts, bad moods, and sulking, which made for a volatile relationship indeed. Another outlet for all this bottled-up emotion was through my increasing sexual promiscuity. I had become consumed by a growing sexual immorality in my life that had gone beyond the explicit magazines and was getting out of control. Even though I was in a relationship, my friends observed my increasing selfish behaviour and how I would not care about picking up and discarding women.

One day, in a surprising outburst of emotion, I was wrestled to the floor, pinned down, and threatened by my close friends to stop and change my promiscuous my behaviour. I didn't realise it at the time, but they were trying to help me from getting into deeper trouble; where they had joked and talked about doing things, I just went ahead and did them. This was not my overconfidence but more of a rebellion borne out of my emotional turmoil. I would do what I wanted, with who I wanted, and not worry about the consequences. The sexual addiction was becoming overwhelming.

Another addiction that was growing out of control was to alcohol. I had started drinking at the age of fifteen. I thought nothing of a little drink at any time of day. It numbed the pain. When my parents were going out, I would invite friends round at home, and we would drink beer and spirits. My father once commented about coming home at the end of an evening out and getting his socks wet as he walked across a carpet which was soaked with beer. I also drank with friends after our weekend rugby matches. After the game, we would call at the store to buy cider and drink it as we walked home and now, in my first job at the bank, I had found a group of friends who found excessive drinking acceptable and normal. Some of these friends also drank daily and in excessive amounts. There was a culture of going to the pub at lunchtimes and then again in the evenings. It seemed that work life and social life had all merged into one. This was becoming a serious problem, although I didn't see it. I thought it was all just simple fun.

The years running up to my eighteenth birthday were becoming increasingly volatile at home. My parents seemed to be arguing more, and there appeared to be a growing undercurrent of unhappiness. I was becoming more selfish, concentrating on my booming social life, and allowing the rift between me and my parents to grow. I found it increasingly difficult to interact with my father. I couldn't talk to him and felt that he was trying to control me. He would shout at me and try all sorts of emotional blackmail on me to get his way. In my father's eyes, I was completely falling off the rails and was on the road to self-destruction; he had no control over the way I was headed. He did what he could to try and get me to change direction, things like locking me out of the house or refusing to let me borrow the car to curb my increasingly volatile behaviour. This resulted in regular arguments and shouting and I thought the best thing for me to do was to spend the least amount of time at home and get out of this environment that was making me increasingly unhappy.

At this time, I had become good friends with one of the managers at work, who, seeing the turmoil in my life, helped me to get a flat to rent in the city. This flat appealed to me for a number of reasons. Firstly, it was about twenty minutes closer to work, so the commute would be easier. Secondly, life would be much more peaceful without all the arguments. Thirdly, I could be my own master; this was quite exciting but also quite daunting at the same time. Yes, the flat looked like a good alternative, and I ignored all the reasons not to take it.

My decision was made, and I was excited, but thinking about the actual process of leaving home made me anxious. It was such a volatile environment; anything could happen. I knew that it was going to be a difficult discussion at home and wasn't sure how it would play out, so I decided to get my things out of the house unnoticed. I thought the best thing to do would be to gradually move out what I needed and then, when I was ready, face the confrontation that would come when I announced that I was leaving.

I started to move my things out from home covertly. Each day, I would go to work and throw some extra clothes into the boot of my car. Then, after work, I would go to the flat, leave clothes in the wardrobe, and come home. I repeated this process daily until my wardrobe at home was quite empty.

I had managed to move out most of my things unnoticed (later on in life, when talking about this, my mother said that she had thought my wardrobe had looked like it was getting emptier each time she put away my washed and ironed clothes). All I had to do now was to wait for the inevitable argument where there would be a suggestion that I should move out.

Sure enough, one evening, the argument came. As expected, in anger and frustration, my father said that I should leave home, and I surprised everyone by agreeing that it was a good idea. I was told that I was allowed to leave home with one suitcase of stuff. I obediently filled a case with the remainder of my clothes and packed some of my other items into my car, ready to leave. Everyone was unaware that I had somewhere to go and thought it would blow over as usual, but not this time.

It appeared that everything was going well; the car was loaded, and I had somewhere to go … that is, until it came time to say goodbye to my brother, Sam. Suddenly, I was struck with an indescribable amount of hurt as I went to say goodbye to four-year-old Sam. As I said before, we had forged a very strong bond between us, and I loved him dearly. As I headed to the door, Sam bounded up to me in his paisley pyjamas to say goodbye.… just like any other night, thinking I was going out and that I would be there in the morning for him to play with. He was oblivious to the fact I was leaving for good. I, on the other hand, was overcome by the searing pain of leaving him. I remember starting my car up in the dark evening, crying my eyes out as he waved from the lounge window. This really hurt and as I drove away, watching him wave in the distance, my heart was torn in two. The pain ran deep inside me, and it would hurt for many years to come.

Throughout this time of growing up, there was no God for me. I had taken A levels at college, and one of them was in computers and programming. I had emerged as a logical thinker and therefore always reasoned things out through a structured thought process. In my younger years, there had been no family member or friend who had encouraged me to have a faith of any type; no one seemed to believe. My parents did go to church for a short period of time, but that fizzled out quite quickly.

I reasoned that because I had also been through so much pain and turmoil in my life so far, there couldn't be a God. I had never seen any evidence of involvement from a higher order; I had not been looked after. The lack of evidence for God was overwhelming. I had absolutely not observed a single thing that even hinted at his existence.

As I had grown up, I had friends who were Muslim, Christian, and Jehovah's Witnesses; over time, we enjoyed numerous lengthy conversation about religion. I had developed logical arguments to undermine all that they would say to me, and they really had no answer to some of my compelling arguments. It was plain to me that none of it was real. I was a solid atheist who had formed my opinions from facts and logical reasoning.

You have to remember that this was at a time before the Internet existed, so information wasn't available at your fingertips. You could only base your opinions on your own personal experiences, and research was a much more cumbersome proposition than it is today. On a few occasions, I had robust conversations with Christians, explaining to them how God wasn't real and presenting my argument in a very persuasive manner, all based on the reality of my own experiences to date.

My only encounter with church had been through the Boy Scouts; once a month, I would have to attend a local church service as part of their parade. Like most of the boys there, what the vicar said and did seemed irrelevant to me and was so far away that it had no bearing on my life. Due to the repetitive nature of the service (which followed exactly the same structured format and timings each week), I could time how long was left of the service and find the best places to wander off in a daydream. Clock-watching became the focus of the service: estimating how long was left of this section and how many sections remained, how long did they take and when would we finish? I wasn't the only one; the other Scouts were doing the same. I remember sitting in that church, asking myself, "What is the point? It isn't real." I was doing my duty for the Scouts, turning up to that church, and that was only the reason I was there.

This was an attitude I took into my young adult life. I had applied my logical brain to the task of reasoning it out, and when combined with the lack of evidence, I had only one obvious conclusion: There isn't a God. I had built up a solid atheist outlook. There couldn't be a God because of all the suffering in the world. Surely, if God was real, then then there would be one faith, and we would see daily tangible evidence of his existence, not confusion, different beliefs, and a lack of anything concrete. I knew I was right and had all the usual atheist arguments that were solid, were logical, and couldn't be undermined.

However, things were about to change...............

CHAPTER 2

A Challenge, a Very Bumpy Road, and an Encounter

'Well, Simon, as you have said, you are an atheist and believe that there is no God. On the other hand, I believe there is a God and an eternal life. Now, as we both sit here, one of us is right, and one of us is wrong. Agreed? Okay, then, if you are right, it will mean that I have spent my life loving people and helping them out, and I will be happy with that when I die. However, if I am right, and you are wrong, then you are in real trouble."

These were the words that had stopped me dead in my tracks. My girlfriend, Julie, had taken me to a vicar's house. She was a Christian, and so too were her parents. I had been seeing her for a while, and they were desperately trying to get me to change my atheist ways, but I was having none of it.

I was still living at home and had met Julie on a night out around the pubs and bars. Despite her saying she went to church, to me, she had appeared pretty normal. You see, I had an expectation that anyone who said they went to church would not be normal. I thought they wouldn't drink or do half the things that I would do. However, this girl appeared to be normal; she had a few drinks and generally did the same things as me. There was no strange religious behaviour I could see. The only noticeable difference was that she would occasionally attend church.....somthing which she had tried to get me to do also but had been unsuccessful in convincing me to go. On one occasion though, I did agree to try it, more so to put a stop to her nagging as opposed to me wanting to go. So, as promised, one Sunday morning, I arrived at their local church in order to attend a regular service. It was a reasonably old building, probably a few hundred years old, a pretty standard affair with large stained-glass windows, a steeple, and a graveyard. However, having entered the church and taken my seat, I found that I couldn't settle. I didn't feel comfortable being in that environment, and the whole experience just made me feel unwell. I was shaking and in a cold sweat. Something inside told me to get out of there, and I wasn't going to settle until I did. I held out until the end of the service but headed straight for the door immediately afterwards. The moment I got outside the church building, I felt better, and normality returned to my life.

What was normality for me? The experiences of my childhood had left me with a real feeling of insecurity, and I carried around a lot of anger inside. The truth was that I was a real emotional wreck and avoided all things that would expose my deeply buried feelings. I was used to just getting on with life and burying all my emotions deep inside. When it came to relationships, I continued to accept being told what to do. For me, this was the easiest option: let someone take the lead. It had happened at home, and I was allowing it to happen in my relationships. I am not sure if my girlfriend had worked this out, but I was doing quite a good job of allowing her to dominate me and getting her own way. I had grown up having a severe lack of confidence, and it was normal for me to take a more comfortable back seat in relationships: less risk.

True to form, I had slipped into my normal subservient role, and everyone thought that I was happy taking a back seat, but the truth was that all was not well. I was not happy. The situation at home was getting to me, and these buried feelings were eating away at me. Whilst I allowed myself to be dominated by those around me, I felt increasingly angry and rebellious. I wanted to react but didn't know how.

I was torn; on the one hand, I had no confidence, and my insecurity meant that I defaulted to allow someone to take the lead, but on the other hand, I was angry at being told what to do. What a mess I was in. It is safe to say that I wasn't in any mood for any discussion on something that would bring added control to my life, such as religion.

But here I was, 1986 and in the house of a vicar, who had just made a statement that for some reason had unsettled me. I had taken 'A' level computing at college. This meant that I was a very logical thinker, always reasoning things out to a sensible conclusion by going through a process of elimination. I had already logically processed the existence of a God and had logically concluded that he didn't exist. I had friends who were Muslim, Jehovah's Witness, and Christian, and I had been through the same debate with them. This vicar was just another one of those conversations. I reasoned that I was right because I had not seen any evidence that God was real. As I hadn't seen any tangible, hard evidence of a real God, this vicar must be wrong. I asked him for the evidence, and he kept talking about things that happened two thousand years ago that seemed irrelevant and unreal to me.

This kind of response does not usually work with atheists, who are always looking for proof and always have an answer to what has been said. I had been in this situation a few times before and prided myself in my compelling argument as to why there was no God. So, in my usual arrogant way, I dismissed what had been discussed. The vicar offered no compelling evidence that God was real. However, there was one niggling thought at the back of my mind that I couldn't shake. He seemed to have absolute conviction that he was right and had repeatedly asked me if I was confident in my thinking; one of us was wrong but who? For some reason, this had struck a chord.

This all happened while I was eighteen years old and still living at home. It was a time when the arguments at home were increasing in frequency and intensity. Most nights at home would invariably involve some sort of shouting and falling out over the lifestyle I was leading; my father and I disagreed on most aspects of life. By now, the house constantly had an atmosphere, and I felt like I was walking on eggshells all the time. Everything I did or said seemed to be wrapped up in the worry of what reaction this would provoke at home. It was a toxic environment. I thought that the best thing to do was to spend the least amount of time as possible at home and get out of the house as often as I could. I found that there was a fine balance to how much time out of the house I could get away with before making things worse. I needed to spend just enough time at home to keep things ticking over but I really wanted to be out and about away from that environment, which was eating me up.

One of best ways to get away from the house and get some peace and quiet was to go to my girlfriend's house. This became a regular nightly event. After work, I would go home, eat, help my mother wash the pots, and run out the door for the rest of the evening until eleven o'clock, which was the time I was instructed to be home for. This eleven o'clock curfew was always a rush, and I often ran very close to it, as I maximised as much time out of the house as possible.

One particular evening, I was very late and because I returned well past the time I should have been back home, my father had locked me out. Having parked my car on the drive and finding that the door was locked, I started to bang on the door so someone could let me in, but no one came to answer. After a short while, I resigned myself to the fact that I would have to sleep in the driver's seat of my car on the steep driveway. I settled down in my car, put the seat as far back as it would go, and closed my eyes. My mind started to whirr, thinking about the situation I was in. What if the neighbours saw me in the morning? What would my parents say? What reaction would I get for being late? I was getting more and more agitated and unable to sleep.

As time ticked by, I realised that not only was I restless with worry, but it was also getting cold. I tried to shrug it off and wrapped my arms tight into my body to increase the heat, but it wasn't enough. I didn't have a coat or a blanket; I had nothing to keep me warm. I couldn't even start the engine to put the heater on because this would disturb everyone and draw attention to me.

So after some time of trying to wrap up and keep warm in the few clothes I had, I decided that enough was enough. I was going inside that house, one way or another. In the quiet of the early hours, I began banging and kicking on the door with increased vigour. I knocked and kicked harder and harder. Either the door would break down or someone would have to answer. Eventually, my mum came and let me in – probably because she was embarrassed of what the neighbours might think. She didn't say anything, just opened the door with a sad look on her face and walked back upstairs to bed.

It was against this backdrop of continuous argument, anger, hurt, and resentment that I had a very strange experience that would short-circuit the logical computer in my brain. It was a typical day, just like any other. There had been the usual arguments at home, and I had left the house in favour of spending time in Julies's house. As we sat in the lounge, I suddenly saw my father pull his car up outside and get out. My heart jumped with an increasing anxiety as he started to walk up the driveway of their home. What was going on? What would happen? Would this be a big showdown?....... I was working up into a frenzy.

My girlfriend's dad went out to confront him, and an argument erupted at the front of the house. Julie promptly followed her father outside. I suddenly found myself alone in their lounge as the commotion outside continued to increase. I was afraid as to what was going to happen next or what I should do.......did I stay put in that lounge or should I go outside? I was desperate and at a complete loss as to the next step.

Suddenly, in shear panic and desperation, I looked upwards and uttered these words: "Jesus, if you are real then turn this situation round. Make it peaceful and send my dad home."

I had no expectation that anything would happen, it was just a cry of desperation, so what came next took me completely by surprise.

A vortex of complete calm and peace descended from the top of my head all the way down to my feet. It was like someone had poured warm water over me. This warm water was running down my body but seemed to be running down the inside of it too, yet I was perfectly dry. As it descended down, I was overwhelmed by the peace that I felt. This was a peace and warmth that seemed to engulf me completely. Every part of my being, every molecule soaked up what was poured over me. It ran deep. As it reached my feet, it felt like there was some sort of barrier between me and the rest of the world. I was in a cocoon of peace and warmth and I felt overwhelmed with love. I was completely separated from the lounge and the world around me. I was utterly immersed in something and disconnected from everything else. It was as if I was being hugged in some huge arms of love.

I basked completely in this cocoon, which lasted a few minutes. It seemed timeless, and I wanted to stay exactly where I was, but it slowly started to lift, first from my feet and then working upwards. As it lifted, the peace and warmth were left behind. I was completely calm and overwhelmed with peace.

Once my senses had re-engaged with my surroundings, I started to look outside to see what had happened. I was shocked; my father had got back in his car and started to drive away. Wow! I now knew in no uncertain terms that God was real. I was utterly stunned and in shock, and I think my uncharacteristic behaviour over the next few hours was put down by others to the circumstances of what had just happened with my father on the drive. No one was aware what had happened to me, and I didn't share what I had just experienced with anyone. I was still in shock and trying to make sense of it all. My logic had just been turned upside down and in such a beautiful and powerful way.

Over the coming days, I remained silent about what had happened, and life continued on with the usual turmoil. The reality of daily events started to become more prevalent in my thinking, pushing the memory of this encounter further to the back of my mind. As time progressed, what had happened got increasingly distant in my memory. I never forgot my encounter and periodically recalled the day's events so that I could ponder over it some more. However, it was something that remained in the back of my mind, pushed there by me allowing the issues of daily life to dominate my thinking. It had been a powerful encounter, but I had not allowed it to bring much change to my life. I continued on as normal. In fact, my behaviour would get worse over the coming months.

However, despite carrying on as normal, this encounter did introduce three changes in my life: Firstly, I stopped saying that there wasn't a God. I now agreed that he existed, but I wasn't going to pursue any religion. I didn't call myself anything, not an atheist nor a Christian. I neither denied him nor followed him. That was a big change for me.

The second change was that I now knew he was listening. I was uneducated in anything religious and didn't know how this worked, but my logical brain had deduced that because he had answered me that day when I cried out to him, then he must have been listening. It therefore made sense to me that when I got in difficult circumstances again, I could cry out to him. Based on this thought process, occasionally I would call on the name of the Lord for help. No continuous prayer, just call on him when needed because I reasoned that he was listening.

The third thing that changed was that I got myself a copy of the Bible. It was only occasionally that I would read a small part of it, but at least I was starting to read some of God's word. I tended to read it when I felt lonely or afraid. There was no reading plan, no daily reading or study guide. One particular evening, I had been out to see a horror movie. I had come back to the flat alone and tucked myself up in bed. The demons from the film kept appearing in my mind and haunting me and despite all my attempts to think of other things, I couldn't sleep. I felt alone and scared and decided to read a quick few verses of my Bible to see if it would calm me down. I reached across to pick it up, and as I did, I dropped it on the bed. It bounced on the quilt and fell open. I looked at the verse where it had fallen open; it was Psalm 88. Was this coincidence or was this God? I was unsure, but the verse seemed to resonate with my struggles. Verses 3 to 5 reflected how I felt in my rejection and unworthiness that I carried from childhood.

> I am overwhelmed with troubles
> and my life draws near to death.
> I am counted among those who go down to the pit;
> I am like one without strength …

These three things were the only changes that this encounter brought. They were not all consuming. The biggest difference it had made was the change in direction of my beliefs. For me, that was pretty big and represented enough change for me at this time. I wasn't prepared or ready to make amendments to other aspects of my life, even though they often resulted in me getting into further difficulties. I was now aware of God but was not ready to change my lifestyle just yet. I continued with the drinking as before. I had no reason to change, and so the thought that God was real was boxed up and put in the corner of my mind. Little did I know what was coming next and that I would have to open up the box I had firmly closed up and packed away into a distant corner of my mind.

CHAPTER 3

The Storm Gets Darker, but There Is a Light in the Clouds

It was 1988, and the first night in my one-bedroom flat brought mixed emotions. On the one hand, I was excited at the freedom and the prospect of a hassle-free life that this new independence had brought me; I could do whatever I pleased, coming in as late as I wanted and going out whenever I chose. I felt that life was much more peaceful because there wasn't a constant atmosphere in the air caused by continual argument; there was just peace and quiet. On the other hand, I was fearful of what the future held; I wasn't confident and in the past always had people around me to direct me. I could find people to do this at work, but that was only one part of my life. For the first time in my life, I felt that I had control of my future. I was truly the master of my own destiny; it was up to me, and it scared me.

At home, I had been used to living in well-furnished and comfortable surroundings. With the flat, I was disappointed and disheartened with the poor quality of the room. It was a single attic room in an old house that needed a lot of love and attention. My room was just large enough for a single bed, wardrobe, chest of drawers, small chair, and a coffee table. It had a small window, and the poorly decorated room had a large very well worn mat on bare floorboards. The kitchen and toilet were shared facilities and were located on the floor below me. The kitchen was sparsely equipped, and I had to keep most of my utensils in my room. All this was an added inconvenience, but it was all I could afford.

There was another tenant in the room below me. He was quite an old guy who hardly spoke any English. He would go out to the local club and come in late at night. Sometimes, he would forget to close the front door. Occasionally, he would make himself toast on the grill pan of the cooker and forget to turn the grill off. I was often woken up by the smell of burning, and when I went to investigate, I would find the empty grill pan, glowing red. I was concerned that the whole place would go up in smoke, with me in it. No, I didn't feel safe or secure.

I was scared of being on my own and felt very lonely that first night. I was tucked away in that attic room, out of sight and sound of everyone else. I spent most of the night listening to every noise in that old house. Across the landing, opposite my door, was another attic room. This was used as a storeroom by the landlord. I could hear creaking coming from behind the closed door, and it is was accompanied by scratching; was it animals? Was it something else? Listening to the noises around me would become a regular feature of my bedtime in my new home. Laying there in the darkness, I would continue to feel lonely and afraid for many nights to come. Despite all of this, the room represented my argument-free, independent space where I could be who I wanted. There was just one problem: I wasn't sure who I was. My life seemed to consist of my continued stumbling from one crisis to another, with no direction and no plan.

Having moved into the flat, the rest of my life carried on pretty much the same as before.

I would continue to go to Julie's house, or she would come over to the flat so we could spend time together. Occasionally, I would go to visit my parents and see my brother and sister. I didn't do this as often as I should have, but life was so busy. I remember on one of these visits, my dad was curious to see my new place as he wanted to see what was more appealing than being at home. I was excited to show him my new pad, so I drove him to the flat for a viewing. However, my excitement soon faded when he walked through the door, and I saw the look of disappointment on his face. He was really upset with my poor living conditions (made worse by the fact that I wasn't the tidiest person in the world). He couldn't understand why I had moved there in favour of living at home and asked me to leave the flat return.

But I had started to enjoy my freedom and independence too much, so I refused. He said that I was always welcome home, and I think he hoped that it wouldn't be long before I returned and got out of the mess that I was in. There was one thing he did make me do, though: He made me promise that I would never allow my mum to see the flat and the mess that I was living in….. it would upset her too much, so I agreed.

From time to time, I would also go and visit Grandma and my uncles. They always made me feel so welcome; each time I walked through the door, I would remember all those happy days I has spent there when I was younger. Yes, this was a nice safe comfortable refuge for me to come back to when I was really feeling down and lonely. I could shut the cares and tribulations of the world out behind me, and we could laugh about all the things that I used to do when I was younger. Yes, this was a real comfort blanket for me in the difficult times.

OH MY GOSH! .....IT'S ALL REAL!

After several months of very little difference to my daily routines, some changes started to appear in my lifestyle. I had been going out with my girlfriend for some time, and we decided to get engaged. I now had a fiancée who was expecting an increasing commitment from me. I had gotten engaged to appease her and show some progress in our relationship but had not thought through the implications of what this meant. There would need to be discussions and plans made for a life together: a house, a wedding. I couldn't commit and was in complete denial, constantly dismissing any conversations about my responsibilities and plans. However, this wasn't the biggest change I was about to experience. It later transpired that this was one of the smaller humps in the rollercoaster ride of this new independent life I was embarking on.

My newfound independence provided me with complete freedom over my time. My fiancée had started a job and was now working shifts, which meant that there were days where we could spend time together and there were days when we wouldn't be able to see each other at all. I found that on some days, this left me with time to myself, which I needed to fill. I set out with good intentions: I would start by cleaning and washing clothes and doing the chores that needed doing. Once I had completed them, then I would sit down with a drink to survey with pride the fruits of my labour. I was disappointed. Despite my best efforts, the place still looked unclean. I could clean and do my chores, but I could never make the flat look nice. On top of that, I wouldn't be able to make any radical adjustments to the room, as I had limited space to do anything with.

Gradually, it started to feel like the walls were closing in on me. I felt lonely. Not only was it my home, but I sometimes felt like it was a cage, especially in the summer, when I wanted to be outside in the garden – but I didn't have one. Over time, I found that I couldn't bear spending long periods alone in the flat. I needed to find something to do, to get some company and get me out of that cage.

I was working in a bank during the day, and on my free evenings, to remove the boredom, I started spending a lot of time in the bars around town. It was only when I felt low or a crisis erupted that I read the odd Bible verse and would seek God for help when I needed something. I had God nicely boxed up in the corner, only opening the box in times of need. The rest of the time, he fell out of sight and out of mind; life was for living and living to its fullest. I had years of catching up to do; my friends had been brought up with more freedom to go to pubs before they were legally allowed and seemed to have made more of their lives. I had never been allowed to join in and do the things that they did. It was now my time to get back what I felt had been lost.

I started to feel like I was in a rebellion against what life had dealt me so far: a rebellion fuelled by an insecurity, a lack of confidence, an anger, and a resentment brought about by all the difficult times I had been through during my upbringing. I felt that I had been dealt a tough hand in life, and now was the time to kick out and get what *I* wanted. When I was alone, I festered in these negative emotions and from the loneliness of the flat, I craved some company. I didn't want to be on my own; I wanted to be accepted by people and to feel wanted. To satisfy this craving, more and more often I would go out with different groups of work colleagues and drink heavily, with the aim of becoming the life of the party. I found that through different groups of friends, I could always find someone to go out with, and by displaying ever increasing outlandish behaviour, they wanted me to go out with them.

OH MY GOSH! .....IT'S ALL REAL!

A double life was emerging. On the one hand, I had what appeared to be a normal, stable life with my fiancée, where I struggled with my level of commitment, and on the other hand, I had my wild and exciting separate life of going out and partying. I had numerous circles of friends developing who were taking up increasing amounts of my time. I loved it.

The more I went out, the more people I met, and as time went by, inevitably, I developed numerous relationships with other women. In my rebellion, I was becoming less caring about other people's feelings and was being pulled more into a world of addiction to alcohol and sex. This double life started to get increasingly out of control as I spun a greater web of lies and deceit.

One afternoon, I went to visit my fiancée at her parents' house. In the early evening, I made an excuse that I didn't feel well and needed to go home. Like any caring people, they offered for me to stay overnight on the couch so I could recover, and they would look after me. I said no, explaining that I would be more comfortable and settled in the flat; they were unaware of my ulterior motives. Once I arrived back at the flat, I changed my clothes and went out with a friend to the nightclubs, where I got drunk and picked up a young lady. This type of behaviour was becoming more commonplace, and I was getting totally out of control.

As time rolled by, I started to realise that there were consequences to leading such a demanding double life. Firstly, it was expensive. I was starting to spend more than I earned. I was getting into debt but showed no signs of slowing down; I was having too much fun. Secondly, I was getting a reputation at work for my drinking and womanising. I was going beyond the acceptable limits for a lot of people, and so, some of my friends started to fall away. This was okay to me, though, because I could still go out on my own and get what I needed.

It wasn't too long, though, before it all started to catch up with me. Finances started to get tight, very tight indeed. I had peaked at going out three times in one night, and on more than one occasion, I had stayed up all night. I was getting deeper into debt. This lack of money had given me another reason to go out for longer periods of time: to avoid my landlord, who was chasing me for the rent. Each month when the rent was due, I would become more elusive, paying later and later each time.

On top of this, I was also coming under increasing pressure from my fiancée. She had said 'yes' when I asked her to marry me, and now she wanted to make serious commitments, activities such as setting a date for the wedding and planning to buy a house. I started to feel that everything was closing in on me and that everyone was on my case.

Those emotions of anger and resentment were starting to bubble and surface. At this point in my life, I was a real bag of mixed-up emotions. If you had met me at that time, you would have not seen the truth. You would have thought that I was bold and overconfident. Like many people in similar situations, I had built up an exterior for others to see, like a suit of armour which existed only to stop people getting in and seeing how vulnerable I really was. Not far below the surface was a lack of self-confidence, combined with the need to be liked and accepted. This wrapped up a deeper layer of hurt, rejection and a real lack of knowing who I was.... a lack of identity. The circumstances that I found myself in were squeezing and shaking up all that was inside and causing me to feel more lost, desperate, and anxious.

OH MY GOSH! .....IT'S ALL REAL!

Having had that one previous encounter with God, I now recalled how he had answered me in my despair when I cried out to him. I remembered my reasoning that he must be listening, always listening. So in desperation, I started to cry out to him again. I also started to read my Bible a little more. As well as reading different parts of the Bible, I repeatedly went back to Psalm 88. This was the verse that my Bible had fallen open to on that particular night. It appeared to speak directly to me and strangely somehow made me feel like I was talking to a God in front of me.

> Lord, you are the God who saves me;
>   day and night I cry out to you.
> May my prayer come before you;
>   turn your ear to my cry.
> I am overwhelmed with troubles
>   and my life draws near to death.
> I am counted among those who go down to the pit;
>   I am like one without strength …
> But I cry to you for help, Lord;
>   in the morning my prayer comes before you.
> Why, Lord, do you reject me
>   and hide your face from me?
> From my youth I have suffered and been close to death;
>   I have borne your terrors and am in despair.
> Your wrath has swept over me;
>   your terrors have destroyed me.
> All day long they surround me like a flood;
>   they have completely engulfed me.
> You have taken from me friend and neighbour—
>   darkness is my closest friend.

Gradually, through my reading and increased prayer, I was opening that box in the corner of my mind, the one where I kept God. As I was opening it slightly, I was slowly coming to understand the reality of God's existence. I felt that now, just like that day of my previous encounter, he was listening to what I was saying. It was as if I was developing a greater knowledge that he was real. It was something that was growing in my consciousness. There weren't any strange sensations or anything, just a greater knowledge and acceptance that he was there. I continued to cry out to him and continued to read my Bible. Slowly but surely, my heart started to soften, and I grew a greater awareness of the reality of God.

As a result of this softening, I found that I was starting to care more about people. Over the previous months, I had not been concerned with people's feelings. I had carried on regardless, impervious to how they were impacted by my behaviour. I had been selfish and self-indulgent. However, I was starting to care about people, their feelings, their well-being, and what was going on in their minds. This was a slow change, from the inside out.

On the outside, my behaviour only showed minimal signs of improvement. You would have had to look hard to notice anything different. Most of the work was being done on the inside; a moral battle was starting to emerge in my mind. Things like the drinking and promiscuity continued at the same pace; there was no real change there, but hidden away inside was a tension that was being wound up like the elastic band of a toy aeroplane. I felt it building. I felt my emotions battling. I felt God getting into my mind. Little did I know that the finger was about to be taken off the propeller, and my elastic band would uncoil violently, propelling me to a different place. There were about to be some big lifestyle changes.

PART 2.

I GET RELIGION

CHAPTER 4

An Angel Arrives, and God Intervenes

It was summer of 1986, and it was the third week of my first ever job. I was working for a bank in the suburbs of a city near to where I grew up, and the bank had gathered together all the new recruits from the local areas for a three-day induction course at the Area Office. This was happening not long before that first encounter with God in my girlfriend's lounge and I was still living at home.

The Area Office was part of the main branch in the city; it consisted of a number of buildings. Our meeting was on the fourth floor of the tallest of these buildings. I had arrived there early on that first day, along with a friend I had met a few weeks beforehand. He had joined the bank at about the same time as me, and we sat down next to each other in the large room, awaiting the start of the course. The room had a series of desks all laid out in a U shape, so that the presenter could walk up the middle and address all the attendees face to face. We took our seats near the top of the table so that we would have a good view of everyone else.

People from different branches of the bank were slowly arriving and entering the room, which was gradually filling up with eager and nervous new recruits. The door was constantly opening and closing as a steady stream of people filed in. We continually watched the door, intrigued to see who would enter next and form a quick judgement on what our first impressions were.

The door opened again, and a group of people started walking through the door. Amongst the group was a beautiful young woman who immediately caught my eye. She had blonde hair and beautiful, clear blue eyes. For a second, it was as if time stood still as she walked through the door. I was transfixed and couldn't take my eyes away from her.

As she walked in, I turned to my friend and said, "I am going to marry her."

He knew exactly who I was referring to, and his reply was immediate: "Yeah, right; in your dreams. Two things: Firstly, she is way out of your league, and secondly, have you forgotten about your girlfriend you are getting engaged to?"

He was right on both accounts, especially on the second point, but something had drawn me to her. For the next three days, I continually tried to catch her attention, but it was to no avail; she didn't appear to be interested.

When the three days had concluded, I went back to my local office and soon forgot about her. My mind was overtaken with trying to traverse the twists and turns of my volatile life. Over the next two years, I had got engaged, had an encounter with God, and moved out from home into my own flat. I had become consumed with surviving the daily trials and tribulations of my more-than-eventful life.

OH MY GOSH! .....IT'S ALL REAL!

About two years after that induction course, I was transferred from my small branch to the large office in the city centre. My new job was in one of the more prestigious buildings, from where some of the bank's more complex services were delivered. There were numerous buildings that made up the large city office, and there were a lot of employees spread across them. It didn't take me long to make friends with the louder and more sociable element of the staff. I continued building my social life and reputation for being a party animal at the new office, getting myself known to lots of different groups of people.

As one of the duties in my job, I had to undertake various activities in some of the other buildings. To complete them, I had to visit the huge City Centre branch across the road from the building where I worked. This office was very big and extended across five floors. It was in this building that I found the large staff room where people could go for lunch and watch television. On some of my days at work, I went out to bars for lunch with various colleagues. On the remaining days, when I didn't go out for lunch, I started to frequent the staff room to catch up with the various circles of friends I was making. We could plan the week's entertainment, and I would slowly fill up my diary for both the days and the evenings.

It was as I sat in this staff room one day that it happened: As I sat there with some friends, I suddenly couldn't believe my eyes. The same young woman who had walked into the induction meeting over two years previously had now opened the door and walked into the staff room. She sat down with her friends and started to eat. I couldn't take my eyes off her. I was overwhelmed and mesmerised by her. My heart was racing. I just had to know who she was, her name, where she worked, was she single? I needed to speak to her.

I started to quiz my friends, and over the coming days, I began to get some answers. I managed to find out that she worked on the counter in the City Centre office. Oh, no; this was the one place in the whole building I wasn't allowed to enter. I didn't have access to the counter because it was where all the cash was handled. I could get near to where she worked, near enough to see her in the distance, but I wasn't actually allowed into that area; there was no way to talk to her. The only option would be to try and bump into her in the staff room at lunchtime.

Because of the size of the office and the number of different lunch hours, it was very difficult to bump into her in the staff room. I spent many days camping out in the staff room; it seemed like ages since she had last been in there, but by persisting day after day and trying different lunch hours, I finally saw her again. She sat with her friends for lunch, and I waited. Hidden behind my armour of overconfidence and arrogance, I had no issues with talking to strange women, so it should have been easy to engage her in conversation. I waited until it was time for her to go back to work.

As I waited, I started to get nervous. This was unusual for me. I had buried my lack of self-confidence behind the false armour of an overconfident exterior, and I normally managed to disregard any hint of emotional nervousness. However, for some reason, on this occasion, I felt nervous and had butterflies in my stomach. Despite this, as soon as she got up to leave, I took a deep breath and set off in hot pursuit.

"Hello, good to see you again," I began. "You might remember me from the induction course two years ago in Head Office? I transferred here recently." I thought this was a good opening that allowed multiple options for a good response.

She replied, "No, I am sorry. I don't remember you."

Ouch! What a crash and burn that was. She didn't remember me. I had made no impact on her whatsoever.

As the weeks rolled on, I made it my personal mission at work to frequent the area where she worked so I could keep bumping into her and turn on the charm that had served me so well in the past. The strange thing was that every time I approached the area where she sat, my pulse would race and I would get excited at the prospect of being able to speak to her. What was going on? Why did I feel like this? I couldn't understand it.

Sure enough, after a few weeks, the ice broke, and I struck up a rapport with her. She seemed to be warming to me. We could not always speak because of the restrictive cashier environment, but when we did, I would always try my best to make her smile and laugh. Then one day, I decided I was going to ask her out to a lunch date. Again, uncharacteristically for me, I felt slightly nervous in asking her. Time and time again, I had played it over in my mind: what I would say, her possible responses. I was prepared this time. This nervousness was not my normal behaviour; this type of thing was usually quite straightforward for me but on this occasion it really got to me.

What's more, it seemed that playing out different scenarios only added to my nervousness. Over a number of days, I frequented the counter where she worked, battling through the nerves each time to see if we would be able to speak. Finally, an opportunity presented itself for us to have a few quick words, so I jumped in and asked her for a lunch date.

Her response was quick, and unlike the painful crash and burn of my first encounter, I was relieved when she said 'yes'. It seemed that I was on to a good thing. A date and time was set, a bar not far from the office. I would collect her, and we could walk up together.

The day couldn't come round soon enough for me. Despite my very busy social life, this was the highlight of the week. It seemed like a long time coming, but finally the day arrived, and as planned, I appeared in her office to collect her. As we walked up to the bar together, we started to have our first proper conversation. She told me how everyone had been warning her of my bad behaviour and had encouraged her to cancel our meeting. She had seen the common sense in what they said but for some reason had decided to meet up. They had told her I was engaged and also about my reputation for womanising and all the things I got up to. She explained to me how she didn't usually get involved with people who were in a relationship, but fortunately for me, she had decided to turn up and see how things went.

We had a great time at lunch together. Whilst we ate and drank, I tried to make her laugh as much as I could; unfortunately, it was often at the expense of those around me. I made sarcastic comments about what they were doing and made fun of them. It was a little bit like a stand-up comedian's act, where I was trying to get her to warm to me. As I continued to act like this, something very strange started to happen to me. I hadn't felt it before. I started to feel a growing guilt for my behaviour because I wasn't doing the right things to please God. It was the first time this had happened to me and unbelievably was happening while I was on a first date with someone I seemed to care so much about. How could this girl and God turn up at the same time and mix me up completely?

We returned to work and agreed to meet up again, much to her colleagues' disgruntlement. She seemed to be under a lot of pressure from the people around her not to meet me again. As for me, I couldn't wait for the next meeting; it couldn't come round quick enough. For some reason, I really liked this young woman and felt an affinity towards her.

That first lunch together had left me overwhelmed in more ways than one. I was excited that I had a successful first date with a beautiful young woman and was looking forward to meeting up again. However, I was confused by what had happened to me in the pub. Why had I felt so guilty about my behaviour? Why had I suddenly started to care? Why had God seemed to get into my head as we ate lunch together? I wasn't sure what was going on or why it had happened, but I would soon find out in the coming days.

We had two more dates and then arranged a third. However, it was becoming obvious that this relationship was going nowhere. I was sure that she faced questions at home about why we never went out properly as a couple at night. There was a glass ceiling to any prospective relationship that might develop. I had a fiancée; I had girlfriends … I obviously had issues. This was too much baggage for anyone to cope with and did not represent the start of a healthy relationship. I was totally unaware that the next time we met, she was going to call an end to our meetings and bring to a close any prospect of a real relationship. My circumstances were something she was not comfortable with at all because they went against her own moral standards and all that she believed.

Whilst I did not foresee what she was going to do, I was aware of the fact that this relationship wasn't going anywhere. I was again overcome with my feelings. I really didn't want to lose her; something was different with her that I didn't understand. What was going on? This wasn't me. I didn't suffer from so much emotion. I had a suit of armour that I hid behind; what was happening?

The time for our next meeting arrived. As we greeted each other, it quickly became obvious this was going to be awkward. I needed to speak first before she could say anything, so I jumped in.

My emotion took over as I said, "Since we last met, I have called off my engagement and ceased all other relationships. I want to go out with you. I want a proper relationship with you. I can change my ways."

To say she was surprised was an understatement. She was totally thrown by what had just been said and agreed to continue with our relationship.

At the time, I never gave thought to why things took such a dramatic change of direction. I felt that this was just another set of circumstances that I found myself in. However, as I have looked back at everything that happened to write this book, on reflection, I can see that I was blissfully unaware that this was all part of God's redemption plan. Despite my toxic lifestyle that surrounded our first meeting, there were too many factors working against us that meant this was not just a set of coincidences. We had gone out with each other despite all the circumstances surrounding my life and people who had tried to stop her from meeting me. We were both walking into a situation that we would normally not get into.

In the midst of our first date, I had suddenly developed feelings and emotions that had come from nowhere. On that day at the bar, where we had so much fun, out of nowhere, God had jumped into my head at the same time this girl had jumped into my heart. There were too many unexplained events around my feelings and all the obstacles that seemed to have been easily overcome. I now realise that this had been a huge U-turn in my life. Truly, God had given me a soulmate for eternity.

However, he wasn't done yet. Although I had found a relationship that I was committed to, there were still the finances … or lack of them. He quickly put in place a series of events to start to resolve all my issues.

Remember my bank manager friend who got me the flat? He had now bought a house and offered for me to go and live in his spare room so that I could start to turn my life around. He wanted someone else at the house for security when he was out and for a bit of company when he was in. So it was with great joy that I left that old attic room and swapped it for a more modern back bedroom … rent free.

Sometime after that, I decided that I wanted to marry this love of my life, Sarah, so I asked her, and was overjoyed when she said 'yes'. Sarah knew I needed to save my money and that I was in debt, so she decided to help me with my financial planning; firstly, she took my credit cards away. Shortly after that, I sold my car, and she allowed me to share hers. It wasn't long after all this that I moved into her family home with her parents, so we could save money on food and living, and save money for a deposit on a house.

I was amazed at the kindness this family had shown; they really cared about me. They quickly took me in as a family member, making me feel welcome and at home. There was a good reason for that: They were Christian, and they cared. Sarah's parents were very actively engaged in the local church, and she had come through the ranks of Sunday school, attending the same church since she was a little girl. I truly felt like I had become part of a family and was exactly where I wanted to be.

In a short space of time, the circumstances of my life had taken a dramatic U-turn. I was completely unaware that God had been listening to me crying out to him through Psalm 88 and that he had put a series of events in place to change my life around. It would be later in life that God would show me how he had been there for me through thick and thin. This type of intervention was going to become a recurring theme.

At this point in my life, if you had asked me if I was a Christian, I would have replied 'no', but God was drawing me closer. Up until this point, I wasn't a Christian and wasn't a regular attendee at church. But despite this, God had looked through my sin and shame; he had heard me crying out in to him in desperation for help, and he had answered.

In this new family environment, I started to attend their church. Over the next couple of years, I was drip-fed the Bible through increasingly regular church attendance. I started to see Easter and Christmas as Christian religious festivals and not just for presents and chocolate (even though they were still major parts of the celebration for me). I still drank, I still swore, I still had a worldly view of things, but I started to hear the word of God from the Bible. This was going to have some sort of impact on me; the word of God penetrates the soul, and unknown to me, that is what started to happen. I continued to change for the better.

Even though I was changing, I hadn't felt a personal salvation. I hadn't asked Jesus to come into my life and take over. I had merely slipped into attending church. I would go on a Sunday morning and enjoy the service; I felt good for a few hours, and then life would carry on as normal. I still had God nicely boxed up, but now I would let him out for an hour on a Sunday morning (and sometimes on a Sunday evening if I went to an evening service). That was good enough for the time being. I was keen to move on and get married, and I wanted to get married in a church; was I a Christian now?

I had been in a real mess but had been pulled out of those asphyxiating circumstances to a new and better place. I had come so far and was enjoying the love, sense of belonging, and security of my new personal life. I had started going to church, and my behaviour was changing for the better. God had done so much for me and shown me a new path. You would think that I would have learned from all these mistakes, wouldn't you? Surely I couldn't mess it up again. Or could I?

CHAPTER 5

A Very Rocky Road, but God Is Right in the Middle of It

Our wedding was a great celebration; it was a large event attended by lots of family and friends. We had enjoyed a beautiful church wedding, followed by a sizeable reception in a large hotel. In September 1991, we had got married in style and now moved into our first home. It was a small terraced property in the city suburbs, and we set about decorating it to make it our home.

Money was tight, and the decorating was to be done on a very small budget. In the kitchen, I took the units out of the small space, redesigned it by adding two additional cupboards and refitted it myself with the inclusion of a second-hand oven. This was the largest project that we could afford to do; all other changes were limited to painting and decorating. As money always seemed to be in short supply, I was always looking for ways to earn more so that I would be able to ease the pressure of those ever increasing monthly bills.

After being married a few months, I bumped into an old school friend, Graham, who seemed to be doing well for himself. I hadn't seen him in years, but at the same age as me, he had a nice house and a nice car and went on nice holidays. It wasn't long after bumping into him that he came forward with a business proposition. It was in a multilevel marketing scheme. Normally, I would have been more sceptical about such schemes, but I had known Graham through school, and he did appear to be doing okay. I thought it would be nice to make some extra cash. Graham introduced me to his associate, who was also working in the business and who started to talk about the nicer things in life: dream cars, boats, holidays. It sound too good to be true, but on the face of it, Graham seemed to be doing okay, so I presumed it was a good thing. I was in. I jumped at the chance to be rich beyond my wildest dreams. My wife, on the other hand, chose not to have anything to do with it and was completely against the idea from the start. Similar to many other occasions in life, I should have listened to her voice of reasoning, but I didn't. That stubbornness which had made its way from my childhood won the discussion.

As the months progressed, this new business venture started to take up more and more of my spare time, which meant that I started to spend less time with Sarah. I was becoming consumed by it and was increasingly spending more time and money on it. There was an elaborate mechanism to keep people motivated to build their own futures. This revolved around purchasing a constant supply of books and tapes which were designed to keep your mind concentrated on the business and focussed on success. My wife and others often said that I was being brainwashed, but I disagreed; it was all personal development. After many months of trying to make a success of the business and spending more money than I was actually making, Sarah thought it was time that I gave it up. She started to put increasing pressure on me to stop doing it and to get back to the life we had. However, I was being drawn deeper and deeper into the all-consuming meetings and purchasing the tools to keep myself best placed for success. I would work at the bank in the day, and some nights I would go out to meetings. Some weekends, I would disappear for whole days for meetings. It was starting to take over my life, but I couldn't see it. My life was starting to revolve around this business, which wasn't making any money and was becoming a constant subject of arguments between us.

Remember how I said I was a mixed cocktail of emotions from my upbringing? Well, it was clear from these arguments that I had issues deep down that would occasionally boil to the surface, giving me a real temper. The arguments would be very heated and usually result in me breaking a door or damaging something in the house. I never hit my wife (I didn't believe in hitting women) but instead took my anger out on the things around me. We would start with harsh words that escalated quickly into an argument, and then my anger would take over as I wound up into a real temper.

One day in a blind rage, I kicked my leg clean through a solid wood door. How I didn't break my leg was a miracle, but I did manage to split my big toe open in the process. There was blood pouring from the end of my foot, and I needed to go to the hospital. I sheepishly asked Sarah to take me, but she refused (I don't blame her given what I had been putting her through), so in the end I called my dad who came over and took me to Accident and Emergency. It was clear, though, that I still had a lot of unresolved issues from my childhood which were festering deep down inside me and were being exacerbated by the events unfolding around me.

As well as all the difficulties that we were going through ourselves, my parents had also been having their own issues in their relationship, and we had seen things getting worse between them. In the years to come, my mum and dad would get a divorce, which is never a good thing for children to see happen to their parents, regardless of their age. It certainly had a big impact on my brother, sister, and me. In fact, in the next few years, a series of events would unfold that would result not only in their divorce and my dad leaving the house but in him being alienated from all of us. We wouldn't see him for years to come. This would split the family up, leaving me with very little interaction with any of my relatives, siblings included.

It seemed that layer after layer of hurt, anger, and insecurity were being overlaid on all of those issues from years gone by, and the events I was experiencing now continued to add to them. The concern with my parents was another layer. The lack of money was another layer. The arguments with my wife were another layer. As the layers built up, I began to feel weighed down even further and increasingly insecure. As I battled with all this, something else happened: My nan passed away. It started to feel like no matter which direction I turned in life, there was some pain and difficulty waiting for me. Inside, I was a mess and trying my hardest not to show it on the outside; I tried to carry on as normal, but I don't think I did this very well.

One particular day, Sarah and I were having one of our regular arguments over my involvement in the business. I was due to go to a meeting, and one of my business associates was coming to collect me so we could go together. Shortly before he was due to arrive, an argument had erupted, and it was quite heated; probably one of the worst ones to date. When the doorbell rang announcing his arrival, I went to let him in.

I opened the door and explained, "We are having an argument; could you wait here in the porch? I will be through in a few minutes."

"Sure," he replied, wide-eyed in anticipation as he remained in the porch.

I returned to the room with Sarah, and the argument continued.

She was not happy and shouted, "If you leave this house, I am packing my bags and leaving, never to come back."

She had delivered an ultimatum, and I didn't think she was bluffing. I was stunned. I couldn't risk losing her and so resigned myself to the fact that I wouldn't be going to the meeting. I turned to go and explain this to my associate, but to my complete surprise, he was walking into the room. He had overheard our argument and taken it upon himself to come in and try to intervene, to try and bring some logic to our emotional tirade.

He started to address Sarah by saying the same things that I had been saying for all these months, but this was like a red flag to a bull. My wife blew up and shouted at him to get out of the house. When he tried to continue, she threatened to call the police if he didn't leave. She threw him out, leaving us to try and pick up the pieces and make sense of what next. It felt like the walls were closing in, and soon I would have to make some serious decisions.

This was a defining argument and a difficult place for us to recover from; we were rock bottom, and it was made worse by the fact that I wouldn't give up trying with the business. I was hopelessly brainwashed into the fact that it would resolve all our problems. I just wanted a better life all round and was spending my time and money to try and achieve this for us. The business and my actions had been driving a wall between us. However, as time went by, we found some common ground to build upon, and we continued to try to move forward. Over the next few years, we were blessed with our first child, Alex….a beautiful daughter. This brought a turning point for me. It had been a difficult pregnancy for Sarah, with a particularly hard childbirth. Seeing her struggle through this brought me much closer to her, and when our daughter was finally born, I realised how fragile life was, and my priorities started to change. Up until that point in my life, I had taken everything for granted: health and life itself. The birth of our Alex started to change my outlook. I needed to be a much better person for everyone at home: a better husband and a better father. I needed to start saying 'yes' to the family more and 'no' to the business more often. However, I found that this was easier to say than actually put into practice. It was difficult to change......I was going to need some help.

Despite all the issues that being involved with the business brought, there was one positive that came out of it: I was introduced to a number of Christians who had a deep faith. I started to hear from other Christians how God had been working in their lives and the encounters they had experienced. This started to increase my faith too. It is true what people say: You need to associate with the right people to keep you on the right path.

One of these Christians invited me to a gathering on Sunday morning. Groups of Christians who were all part of the business periodically met in a larger venue, such as a conference centre and an open invite was extended to others in the business. I did accept some of these invites, but I found them to be uncomfortable experiences that were difficult for a number of different reasons.

At the first couple of meetings, I found that I was completely out of my comfort zone. To date, my few experiences of church had all been in a structured, organised meeting that usually followed a familiar pattern. They included reading and chanting the service from books, collective prayer, and a few hymns dispersed at intervals across the proceedings. Despite them being quite dry, there was a safety in my knowing what was going to happen and keeping everything in control. The meetings I had been invited to by my business associate were something completely different.

They were held in auditoriums or conference centres, which was the first time I had seen this happen, I never knew Christians met outside the church. They would start with a welcome, which was then followed by a number of vibrant songs, all accompanied with clapping and arm waving. After this, someone would preach a message including some Bible verses which would then be followed by prayer and finally an altar call for anyone who wanted to accept Jesus as their Lord and Saviour.

I really struggled with those meetings. There was no way that I would show myself up by clapping and raising my hands. I was too sophisticated and sensible for that. I couldn't understand what these people were on, but they seemed to have lost control of themselves, and I wasn't going to do the same.

I only attended a few of these meetings. In the first one, I was shocked at what I saw and couldn't understand it although I did like the speaker's message. At the second one, I found myself crying during the worship; again, I related to the speaker's story, which was very moving. However, the third one was completely different.

The third meeting was in a conference centre not far from where we lived. The format wasn't any different from the previous two; I think God had just been preparing the ground. At this third meeting, God started working on me the moment I entered the building. I felt my heart in my mouth every time I said good morning to people. I couldn't understand what was going on; I was in a heightened state of emotion.

The first song began, and I started to cry. I cried all the way through the worship and found myself crying with my hands in the air. After the worship, God tugged at my heartstrings all through the message that was preached; I had a feeling that something was going to happen. An altar call was made (an invitation for anyone who wanted to accept Jesus as their Lord and Saviour to go the front of the room and pray). As the call was made, I stayed in my seat, watching others get up and make their way to the front. I was in no state to do anything, so I just sat in my seat. As I watched others go forward, my heart started to beat louder and louder, then I felt myself being pulled towards the stage. Before I knew it, I was at the front of the stage, crying. The speaker led us all in a prayer of repentance, and then we all asked Jesus into our hearts and declaring him as our Lord and Saviour. It was a glorious moment as about 120 of us were all saved. There was lots of weeping and lots of celebration.

Even though there was no vortex or encounter like I had all those years earlier, I had still experienced overwhelming emotions and feelings that had taken me over. They had been completely unsolicited and had just happened after the meeting began. I came away from that meeting with an inner feeling that things were different. There was an undeniable reality about what had happened.

There were certain aspects of my life that remained unchanged, for example, the drinking and the swearing. I still desired to do well in life and was still involved in the business. However, over time, there was change happening in other parts of my life. I had a desire to get closer to God and started to read my Bible more. I started to cry out more in my times of need, which were becoming more frequent. I also wanted to go to church and fellowship with others. One of the other local business associates saw this and invited me to go to his church one Sunday morning. I accepted.

As agreed, one sunny Sunday morning, I went along to his church, meeting him on the way so that I wouldn't get lost. We walked through the doors of the modern building and into a large room. It was a very light and airy room, and people seemed to be very welcoming. There was no organ, but there was a band and an overhead projector for words. Some of the floor had seating; some was left empty. It was a very strange setup, not like any church building I had seen before.

The band struck up into vibrant worship, and people started clapping their hands and banging on percussion instruments. Some started to wave flags and dance. One chap had a staff with sleigh bells on it, and he was shaking it and banging it on the floor. I started to feel very uncomfortable and believed that to others I looked completely out of place. As the worship went from one song to another, some people started making strange sounds and speaking what appeared to be gibberish (later, I would come to learn that they were speaking in tongues).

I was finding it difficult to connect and engage in the service. I thought it all seemed to be unorganised and a little chaotic. As some people stood and some danced, others took to laying on the floor. I didn't know what to do with myself. The worship was followed by some teaching from the Bible and then a time of prayer. Shortly afterwards, the service drew to a close, with an offer of further fellowship and refreshments. At the end of the service, I couldn't get out of the building fast enough. I made my excuses and headed out of the door. It had been a really uncomfortable experience for me.

I never went back to that church. I couldn't handle it and certainly didn't understand it. Instead, I started to visit a few different churches locally, but I couldn't seem to find a place where I felt comfortable. After trying a few, I found a local church that I felt happy enough with, attending infrequently on a number of occasions. Ironically, it was the nearest church to our house, but I had often passed it by, thinking that it looked dark and uninviting. The church building was old, centuries old, but I found the service was a mix of traditional and contemporary styles, which suited me better. I seemed to settle a little more there here than I had anywhere else locally (the best church for me was the one that my in-laws attended, but this was reserved for the times when we would visit for a weekend).

Another reason for me attending this local church was that I bumped into someone I had met previously. Remember the vicar who had challenged me all those years ago? Well, his wife was a regular attendee at this local church and was an active member of the small congregation. Unfortunately, her husband had died some years before. The moment she told me he had died, I couldn't stop thinking about that conversation we had all those years ago, especially the part about what would happen when we died. I smiled about the fact that I had realised in the end he was right and I had been wrong. Bumping into her after all those years seemed to solidify my faith even more by bringing back to mind the events of that time. I did wonder if God had designed that my path would cross with the vicar's wife in order that he could affirm my faith by reminding me of that encounter with him all those years ago.

Slowly but surely, my faith was growing, and I would pray more often. Through these recent events, God had brought back to the forefront of my mind that encounter from years ago. This in turn had given me a renewed revelation that he wanted to be actively engaged in our daily lives. I hadn't recognised this before; it was something new that God had shown me through this recent encounter with the vicar's wife. Years ago, God had used this vicar to challenge me, a stubborn atheist. That challenge had been sufficient to cause me to call on the Lord all those years ago when I needed him. Now, I realised that because God responded all those years ago when I cried out to him, and now again by bringing the vicar's wife to a nearby church, he continually desired to be involved in my life.

I was completely overwhelmed by this concept of involvement and found it difficult to comprehend. I mean, from speaking to other Christians, I had found out how he had been involved in their lives too. I couldn't get my head round how he could be involved in billions of people's lives all at once. It was this concept that I really struggled with. The cynical old atheist mindset was a difficult one to get rid of. There was a battle underway in my thinking as to how God could possibly be involved with billions of people, and for what purpose? Why would he want to be involved in our lives? I was contemplating all of this in my head, over and over unaware that I would soon get an answer to both these questions.

Our house had a large attic room which I had utilised as an office/spare bedroom. I had put a big desk in it, and some nights, I could be found up there, working and planning. One particular Thursday evening, I was in the attic about eight o'clock. I was writing some notes for work when I was suddenly overcome by the desire to go to the house two doors down from ours. *Very strange*, I thought and carried on working. Seconds later, I was again overcome by this desire to go to the neighbour's door.

I shook it off and carried on writing. Again, seconds later, I was overcome by the same desire, but this time, it intensified. I had to go. I put the pen down, got up from my desk, and descended the two flights of stairs to the ground floor, where I said a very strange thing to my wife: "I am just popping next door but one. I am not sure why but will be back soon."

She acknowledged me, and I headed out of the front door.

I arrived at our neighbour's door and knocked, not knowing what I was supposed to say or do and not sure why I had called on them. I knew the husband and wife who lived here, but this could be embarrassing. I knocked, pondering what I would say, when all of a sudden, the wife opened the door and startled me by saying, "Thank God you have come. I have been praying that you would come round."

I was utterly stunned. I couldn't comprehend what she meant, but that feeling was short lived when she uttered her next words: "My husband has been drinking, and he is in the front room with a knife, threatening to commit suicide."

I entered the house and headed into the room. After chatting with him, I managed to talk the husband into giving up the knife. We then spent some time talking the situation through until he saw things in a different light. I wasn't trained in what to say, but one of the profound things that helped him was when I described what had just happened to me. I explained that God loved him so much that he had sent me round to help.

That was the answer to my questions. God *is* involved in billions of people's lives all at once. How does he do it? I don't know, but it didn't matter that I didn't know how anymore because I had seen it for real. Why does he get involved? It is because he loves us and desires to interact with us. I had learned something from all this and it was this; that God was a very practical God and was looking for people he can use on a daily basis. This was the first of many times that God would show me something by making it happen.

Let's pause for a moment and take a look at the events in this chapter through my old atheist eyes so that we can reflect and logically think through what had happened…. after all that was the approach I had constantly taken to disprove God's existence all those years ago; An easy argument would have been that this was all coincidental. This is an argument I had used many times before. In the conference centre that day, it is easy to see how I could have been carried along by everyone else's emotion. And giving my life to the Lord and crying? Again, I could have been steered by the speaker to walk to the front and allowed the emotion of my surroundings to carry me. What about bumping into the vicar's wife at the church near my house? This could just have been coincidence; I was reading too much into it! The scenario with the neighbour? Purely circumstantial; I knew them, and again, I was making it sound like something more than it was.

Previously as an atheist, I had taken pride in the logic and prowess with which I had presented my arguments and undermined my opponent's lack of evidence. However, I was finding that having experienced these situations for myself, I would be hard-pressed to apply these arguments to what had happened to me. Firstly, there was no motivation for the folk at the meeting to lead me into becoming a Christian. I mean, I never met any of them after that event, so what did they gain from it? Also, because I found the environment uncomfortable, I was purposely disengaged from all the singing and dancing from the outset and so was not involved in the emotion. What actually happened was on the inside of me and started long before the speaker uttered his first words.

As for bumping into the vicar's wife at the church nearest to my house? That was too close for a coincidence and at a time when I needed to be reminded of that conversation and my first encounter with God. The neighbour? Well, circumstantial wouldn't be a logical argument. I had tried to dismiss the feeling twice, but the third time, the feeling became overwhelming, and even I questioned why I was doing what I did (I didn't know why I had started to walk to their door). Then, when I knocked on the door, I found that I had felt this way on the back of someone actively praying for me to go round to the house….. No, sorry, the atheist arguments were too weak to explain away what had happened. The logical argument clearly swayed to the fact that it was God taking action. Circumstantial as an explanation simply didn't cut it any more.

If I pause to look at this through the eyes of a Christian, there are a few important points to take note of: In the conference centre, even though I had struggled with the environment, there was a freedom for God to move and touch people. Timings, structure, and constraints had been removed from the meeting. Also, at the end of the meeting, they made a call for people to give their lives to Jesus and be saved….. Oh, the importance of ministry and an altar call, where God can do so much. Finally, the incident with the neighbour showed me that God loves interacting with us and wants to work with and through us; we need to be open to him and willing to serve.

In Exodus 14:16, God used Moses to part the Red Sea:

> Raise your staff and stretch out your hand over the sea to divide the water so that the Israelites can go through the sea on dry ground.

Couldn't God part the Red Sea by himself? Of course he could, but he chose to work through Moses, and therefore Moses had to raise his staff for God to part the sea. What will we allow God to do through us today? Are we bold enough to ask him to show us and then be brave enough to be obedient when he does? Try asking God today: What does he want to do through you? Who does he want you to help? What does he need you to say? It doesn't matter if you don't have everything sorted in life; look where I was when he did this for the first time through me. He wants you to enjoy doing things with him right now, regardless of where you are in life; dare you ask him?

CHAPTER 6

Time for a Change and to Turn up the Light

We had seen the birth of our second child, Thomas a healthy bouncing boy. He was now living in our bedroom with us. The house was becoming more crowded with two adults, two children, and two cats. Ah yes, the cats; I had forgotten to mention them. Prior to our children being born, my wife had been feeling lonely at home and wanted a cat as a pet. I wasn't a great cat person but thought it might be a good idea, as it might help her settle. I dutifully visited a local pet shop to see what they had in store. I was in luck; they had two sisters remaining from one litter. It was obvious that one of the cats was in good shape and so she was the cat I chose. I then looked at the other cat, which was to remain in the pet shop all alone. It glanced at me with its wide eyes and a look that melted my heart. I couldn't leave her behind on her own. I would have to take her too, even though she was clearly the runt of the litter. So there we have it: We had two cats and now two children.

We found that with two children came a lot of stuff, and now the house was getting full. We needed a bigger house but couldn't afford to move. I had been sinking my money into the business and had also splashed out on a BMW, which had become an idol to me. Things had been getting increasingly tough financially, and I couldn't see how we would be able to move.

Sarah was getting unhappy with where we lived and longed to move back to the town on the south side of the city, where she had grown up. The whole situation had an air of desperation and urgency around it because our daughter, Alex, was fast approaching an age when she would be starting school, and we were really keen that she didn't go to the local school. We wanted our children to grow up in a better environment. The area where Sarah grew up in would be ideal. There were a number of parks and good schools and amenities. However, the downside was that this was an expensive place to live, which put the possibility of moving there even further out of reach.

For me, it was like living in the flat all over again, but now with a family who were dependent on me. Even though I was putting on a brave face, I was getting depressed. I started to take vitamin supplements to feel better. I also started to drown my sorrows more often with the help of the home-brewed beer and wine.

All this was taking a toll on me. I remember one weekend how everything got to me. We went away for the weekend to visit my sister-in-law. All the weekend, I prayed that God would let me die and get me out of the situation. I was ready to call it a day; I was overwhelmed by circumstances. This time, I was crying out to God for all the wrong things, not for help but to just take me to heaven. Again, he would answer but not by letting me die; he would answer me the same way as he had done before: with a rescue.

Even though I had been saved and experienced God's reality on those few occasions, I really couldn't see him working in any part of my situation. I had backed myself into a corner, and because it was of my own doing, I felt that I had to try to fix it. I couldn't see that God would want to sort out the mess I had created. I still continued to take a worldly view of everything, always looking for ways that I could resolve situations myself, without anyone's help. I had been pushed into independence at the age of eighteen and fought my way through plenty of difficulties.

Now, again, I would decide the best way forward. My thought processes were sound in respect of wanting to try and work my way out of the situation, but the problem was my execution and that I had continuously made a mess of things. It was plain to see that my track record wasn't that good. I knew it, but because of that tenacity and stubbornness I had grown up with, I refused to listen to the advice offered by those around me who cared. I couldn't see how they could help, and I couldn't see how God could help.

Fortunately for me, my wife, with the help of her parents, persisted and over time managed to make me see sense. She had a solution: We would sell our house and go and live with her parents for a few months so that we could pay off debts and save up a deposit for a house. Then we would be able to buy a house in the area she wanted. We would have more space, and she would be much happier. This would also allow Alex to start in a local Christian school. At first, I was reluctant to do this but eventually agreed, as I couldn't see any alternative. It was then that she played her trump card: As part of the deal, I had to give up the business.

I had been involved with this business for a number of years. I had sunk time and money into it, but as of yet, I was far from making any profit. Why had I continued with it for so long? Even Graham, my good friend from school who had introduced me to it had left to pursue his career. The reason I had stayed was that I was vulnerable and still had that need to belong to something. There had been a lot of emotional mind games played in the business to make sure people would not leave. There were the books and the tapes to constantly penetrate into your mind. Also, the meetings would run for long periods and very late into the evenings….. sometimes into the early hours. I once looked up the definition of a cult and what behaviours and techniques were used to keep members inside the group. I noticed that some similar methods had been used in the business to keep people involved: brainwashing through materials, sleep deprivation, emotional blackmail, and the constant referral back to an ideology…… The dream of better things.

Don't get me wrong; I am not calling it a cult. There was some good positive attitude training in it; I am just saying that there were similarities in some of the behaviours. This was why I had found it so difficult to leave. I had experienced emotional blackmail in my childhood and now felt the same had happened in the business. This had been really damaging to me, my wife, and those around me. I reflected long and hard; leaving the business was a really tough thing for me to do, but Sarah had made perfect sense, and I agreed.

We sold our house and moved everything into storage, taking up residence once again with Sarah's parents. It was just like before. We were again saving for a deposit for a house. I no longer had my BMW that I had idolised, and there was again some security around us. There was an air of a new beginning, I had a sense of freedom as I was released from the oppression of the business and the arguments that accompanied it. This all felt very similar to the previous time we had spent at my in-laws' house.

I was very grateful to them for blessing us. However, this time, there were some subtle differences. Whereas before, Sarah and I had been preparing for a wedding, this time round, we were reconciling and making up for all the difficulties we had been through. I had put her through a lot. Sure, there had been good times, but I had caused her a lot of pain and upset, and there needed to be healing for both of us.

The previous time when I had moved in with my parent in-law's, God had put me in a stable environment with a Christian family so that he could water that seed of faith within me as I embarked on a new journey. This time round, he used this environment to build on my growing faith and bring a healing from recent events and my business experiences. As Sarah's parents were regular church attendees, I too was drawn into attending the local church, which my wife had grown up in. I was now hearing the word of God on a regular basis. It is amazing the impact that just hearing the word of God has on your soul… it is wise, piercing and refreshing.

I started to get more involved with events such as youth church. I enjoyed the sermons, there was an honesty about the teaching which I liked, and the words spoke deeply to me. We were attending the church as a family, and this started to have a positive effect on our relationship. This effect was not only corporate but individual too. As well as everyone growing in their faith, I continued to grow in the knowledge of the Lord. I was fellowshipping in a comfortable environment and in a service that was structured and that I recognised. God was real and was still in the box in the corner; however, it was a bigger box, and the fact he was there would mean that I now recognised him in my daily life. I was becoming a churchgoing Christian and a fully signed-up member on paper. Little did I know what was round the corner and the changes it was going to bring.

PART 3.

THE TRUTH AT LAST

CHAPTER 7

My Train Crashes off the Rails, but God Makes His Big Move

We originally agreed to live with Sarah's family for a few months while we sorted our finances out, and now a year later, I suddenly found myself being driven round the local area by my father-in-law, looking for houses. I had become too comfortable and had showed no signs of moving out of their home. The effort to move me out started one Sunday after church, where he drove me around, looking at different areas and styles of house. This was then soon followed by the appearance of brochures for houses that were up for sale. I took the hint that it was time for us to move and got myself motivated. It wasn't long before we moved into a house that felt like home from the very first moment we saw it.

Money issues had not resolved themselves overnight, and so things continued to be tight. I decided to focus on my career and try to make more money to ease the pressure. Over a short period of time, I moved through various jobs and eventually took a job where I was working away from home three days a week. I would leave in the early hours of Monday morning (sometimes on a Sunday evening) to drive 4 hours to Scotland and come back Wednesday or Thursday night. This would be repeated week after week.

It was really difficult for me to be away from the family and I found the loneliness overbearing; the obvious thing to do was to try and enjoy myself while working away in order to break up the monotony. There was a small group of us working away from home in the same place, and we started to go out to various bars and restaurants at night. This started as something we would do on one of the nights each week, like a reward for all the hard work we did away from home. It didn't take long, though, before it became something we did most nights. Not only did the frequency of the outings increase, but so did the alcohol consumed each evening. I was drinking more alcohol now than ever before.

This increasing social activity was a means for me to break up the loneliness of being away in a hotel room on my own. Having something to drink numbed the feeling of being alone and helped me settle in my sleep. What I was unaware of was my tolerance to becoming drunk was getting higher, and that meant I was starting to drink an increasing amount of beer, wine, and spirits.

It seemed that I had fallen into a cycle of going to church on a Sunday morning, coming home, and feeling better in spirit for a few hours. This would then subside as I got myself back to normal and ready to face the realities of the week ahead. I needed alcohol to get me through the difficulties of both the work and emotion of being away from home. God was nicely boxed up into Sunday morning and was less real to me than everything else going on in my life. Of course I believed, especially with the things I had experienced so far. It was just that the reality of God was outweighed by the realities of having to earn money to support my family. Being away from home so often gave me time to question where my life was headed. As I got up at 4 a.m. on a Monday to take the lengthy journey to work, I would often ask myself, "Is this it? To be travelling around to earn a good salary and spending just a few days at home? Week after week, year after year?"

I felt that I was getting stuck on a treadmill to nowhere, and it was depressing. I had so many years ahead of me still.

My wife was also finding it increasingly difficult with me being away. She had so much to cope with at home as well as working part-time. I wasn't around much at all, and she was like a single parent balancing everything and raising our children. Over time, the pressure started to get to us, and we started to argue. However, this time, I was on her side. I was missing the family and resented being away from home so much. For once, it felt like it wasn't my fault; we were arguing over circumstances as opposed to my behaviour. In the previous years, arguments would have been about my stubbornness in following futile plans. However, this was me caught up with the same circumstances as Sarah; the only selfishness was in the active social life I had while I was away. Previously, I would have been very selfish about doing the things I wanted to do and quite independent in my approach. Things were different now; over recent months, the word of God had been permeating through my entire being from those Sunday morning sermons. I had a greater love for my family now than ever before, and so I decided it was time to find another job.

After a short search, I managed to find another job nearer to where we lived, which allowed me to come home every day. Combined with this, I was making more money, and things seemed to be a little better. I could now take a breath of air because for the first time in my life, I felt less pressured. As I was lavishing in this less stressful lifestyle, everything seemingly in place, Sarah dropped a bombshell on me that would break my peace and tranquillity: She wanted another child.

Whilst many people would be really happy to have a baby with all the joy that it brings, I was totally against the idea. I had a list of reasons why we shouldn't do it: Firstly, we had a healthy girl and a healthy boy … one of each, so we were good. Secondly, we had no spare bedrooms, so would have to move, and we couldn't afford to do that. Thirdly, we had only just got our head above water, and maternity leave combined with another mouth to feed would put additional financial pressure on us. Fourthly, a family of four fit into everything nicely: the house, cars, and holidays. Five meant upsizing everything and increased costs. Finally, I didn't want to risk anything going wrong with my wife's or the baby's health. I was fearful that something was going to go wrong.… this was a feeling that I couldn't seem to shake off. No, this wasn't going to happen, and I stood my ground because logically, it didn't make sense.

About this time, a new minister, Wesley, came to lead our church, and I struck up a really good relationship with him. Wesley had a different approach to the previous vicar, and he managed to draw me deeper into church life. I started to run a youth group, following prescribed materials to make sure that the message was consistent with the church's teaching. Preparing for these meetings exposed me to more of the Bible. This in turn was bringing me to a greater realisation of the reality of God. However, I still kept him nicely boxed up in the corner of my life because I still continued to see that the realities of life were bigger to me than he was, but the box was gradually getting bigger. Keeping him nicely packaged away in the corner, I kept at arm's-length the memories of how involved in my life he had been in the past and how practical he could be. I kept him at arm's length mainly because I was concentrating more in trying to make life work and didn't think his desire to be involved extended to everything that was going on in Simon's world.

Despite constant pleas from my wife, I did not relent in refusing to have another baby. However, as time progressed and God continued to work on me through all those scriptures, my heart started to soften. Then, one day, about a year and a half after Sarah had first mentioned it, we had been out visiting her parents, and as usual, we pulled up in the car at home. As I unlocked the front door to our house, I casually turned to Sarah and said, "In most things in a relationship, you can compromise and find common ground to work things out. In this situation of you wanting another baby, there is no compromise; one of us will have to back down."

She looked at me, eyes widening to see what would come next.

I continued, "So I will back down gracefully. Let's have another child."

I don't think Sarah could believe what she had just heard. Usually, I would never back down on something. God was slowly doing a work in me. It had taken eighteen months for me to agree, but I finally got there. I did still have that niggling feeling that something was going to go wrong. In agreeing to another baby, I did spot a window of opportunity to get something out of it for myself: The selfishness was still there. After very little persuasion, I managed to get Sarah to let me have another BMW.

The next few months were very painful. My wife got pregnant but miscarried, and another baby died during pregnancy. However, third time round, everything seemed to be fine with the pregnancy, and we were on course for a full-term pregnancy. We needed to get a bigger house to accommodate us all, and one month before the due date, we moved into a house with an additional bedroom. After four weeks of intense decorating, we were finally ready for the birth of our third child.

Everything went well with the birth, and we settled into our new home. I started a new job so that Sarah could leave work and look after the children. Unfortunately, over time, I again found myself spending more and more time away, in London. Three to four days a week, I would be in London or another part of the UK. As before, this started to make things difficult at home. Sarah was coping with a new baby and having to do so much in the house. Being away from home so often also resurrected my bad habits. As before, I began to drink more and started to go out to the bars and restaurants of London every night. In fact, the social life away from home was so busy, I would come home on Friday and sleep most of the evening to catch up on my rest for the weekend. After being away all week, just when Sarah would finally get to see me and be looking forward to some family time, I would be asleep and recovering from a busy week, both in and out of work hours. This was starting to impact my home life again.

I continued to go to church and remained good friends with the minister, Wesley. Where I could, I still did things with the youth group, but I couldn't commit to as much as before. I was by now leading a double life that were polar opposites. Needless to say that all the drinking and time away from home was again resulting in an increasing number of arguments. So once again, I changed jobs.

The new job meant that I was home a little more often. I still had to travel to London regularly, and when I did, my drinking and socialising continued. However, I was home more often than in my previous job and was even able to work from home most Fridays. This was a much better position to be in than before and made home life a lot easier.

I was making more money too, and boy, was I spending it. I was still very materialistic. I had a BMW that I idolised. So much in fact that I would take it out of the drive and wash it and then put it back in the garage, only to repeat the same process the week after. I was averaging about four hundred miles a year in the car…. It was a complete and total idol to me. I also enjoyed watches. I had my first Rolex and when my fortieth birthday arrived, Sarah bought me a more expensive Rolex. Material things were a key part of my life. I also loved movies and watching TV. We had five televisions spread throughout the house, and I would watch endless films on them.

However, despite the improvements in our circumstances, things were not well with me, and I didn't know why. I wouldn't commit to church; in fact, I seemed to be withdrawing. I was getting increasingly angry and short tempered. There was a lot of shouting going on at home, mostly coming from me and directed towards Sarah and the children. The smallest things would wind me up and cause me to shout. I couldn't understand why I was getting so wound up. On many occasions, Wesley would ask me what was wrong and why I wouldn't commit to things as much as I used to. He used to say that Jesus loved me and was there for me.

Over a number of months, I would often reply, "I know Jesus loves me. However, the best way to describe how I feel is this: I can see Jesus stood on his straight path just over there, beckoning me to come and walk with him. For some reason, I am angry and kicking up the dirt in the field, refusing to get on the path with him. I just want to stay here kicking the ground in anger. I don't know why; I just do."

This carried on for many months, and then one Saturday evening, we were invited to Wesley's house for a meal. It wasn't unusual for us to go over for a meal or for them to come and eat at our house. We all seemed to get on quite well, the adults and the kids too. This particular Saturday evening was to be a child-free event, just me and Sarah and Wesley and his wife. After a delicious meal, we sat in the comfort of the lounge and started to chat about things. It didn't take long before the topic got around to the difficulties we were experiencing at home.

All of a sudden, Wesley turned to me and asked, "Well, Simon, how do you feel?"

As soon as he finished asking the question, I burst into tears. I couldn't stop. It went on for some time, and in the midst of all the crying, I managed to utter these words: "Our baby died."

At that moment, the reason for my anger became clear. I hadn't been aware that this had impacted me so much, but I was crying uncontrollably. I was struck with grief.

This emotional outburst helped me and everyone to understand what had been driving my behaviour. Was I healed of the hurt and anger? No, I wasn't. I would continue to be short tempered at home, and life would carry on as normal, only with a bit more understanding of why I was acting like I was. However, during the times of my remorse, I would start to cry out to God to come and help me. I was hurting, hurting a lot and the crying continued. I didn't want all this pain and upset. I now felt that the event of losing two children had resurfaced all the emotions from the years of my childhood. The pain and suffering of my past seemed to be rising up from deep within me and oozing out of me with an anger I couldn't control. This was why I was stood in the field kicking the dirt and why I refused to get on the path with Jesus.

OH MY GOSH! …..IT'S ALL REAL!

A few months rolled by, and now it was mid-December 2006, just before Christmas. The trees and decorations were up, the preparations for festivities were under way, and in the middle of a normal run-up to Christmas, coming completely out of nowhere, something happened. I was suddenly overcome and totally consumed by a desire to see the film *The Passion of the Christ*. This film had been around for a couple of years and was a graphic recount of Jesus's crucifixion. I had heard about it from other people who had seen it, but it wasn't a film I had ever really wanted to watch. Now, for some reason, I had an overwhelming desire to watch it. It was a desire that seemed to be eating away at me daily. It was similar to that time when I was in the attic and overcome by an uncontrollable desire to go to the neighbour's house, only this time, it was to watch a film. Was I going mad? Regardless of what I thought, the compulsion continued to grow daily.

In the end, I succumbed to the increasing desire to see the film. I bought a copy of the film on DVD. No one else wanted to watch it, so I would be watching this one on my own. I waited for a convenient time to put it on, alone in the lounge. Whenever a window of opportunity to be alone presented itself, I would put the DVD into the player and settle down to watch it. However, each time I did, no sooner had I sat down to watch the movie when someone would come to disrupt everything: Either a Christmas well-wisher would call by or the phone would ring. It seemed that every time I planned to sit down, some event would disturb me, preventing me from even turning it on. The desire to see it grew, and it wasn't until the week after Christmas that I would finally get to watch it.

I managed to carve out some time where I could sit down alone in the lounge and put the film on. This time, there was no interruption, and I watched the film all the way through. Probably similarly to many people who have watched that film, I was horrified at the depiction of what Jesus went through and found myself crying on more than one occasion at what I was seeing. Such grace and mercy but also such a passion to complete the job of saving humankind.

After the film ended and the credits were rolling. I was weeping and blowing my nose, trying to compose myself, when all of a sudden, I heard a voice say, "I did that for you; now, what are you going to do for me?"

I was stunned. Had I really just heard that? I couldn't comprehend what had just happened. Suddenly, the top of the box in which I had conveniently packaged God was completely blown off. For the next few days, I couldn't stop those words blazing through my mind, piercing my heart, and permeating every molecule of my being. What did this mean, and what could possibly happen next?

CHAPTER 8

Clear out Your Baggage: Time for a Crazy Life with God

After watching the film, the service at church the following Sunday was different from all those I had been to before. The format and the structure was the same and followed the usual pattern; the difference was with me. I walked into the building as normal, but things felt different. It felt as though there was only Jesus and myself in the room, and from the very beginning, every prayer, song, and word spoken, everything that happened, was personal and a direct interaction between me and Jesus. Ignoring everything around me, I walked to the front of the church and knelt at the foot of the cross. I wept and repented of my behaviour and my sins.

Again, I was enveloped in a vortex of peace, just like all those years ago when I had cried out to God. I stayed at the foot of the cross for some time, as the Lord did a great work in me, delivering me of all my emotional turmoil and hurt. At the end of the service, I left the church forever changed; it was so powerful and seemed to run deep inside me.

Later that week, I was chatting with Wesley about the Sunday morning service; he was inquisitive as to what had been going on. He knew of all the circumstances around my life and the struggle that I had been going through. I told him how I had been compelled to watch the film and what Jesus had said to me at the end of it. I then told him what had happened in the church service that Sunday.

I explained, "As I walked into the building, it was as if Jesus was waiting for me to enter the room. As the service progressed, it became a personal one-on-one between myself and Jesus. I became less aware of those around me and more aware of Jesus in front of me. Every word of every song that I sang was personal, in that I was singing them directly to Jesus."

"I noticed something was different when you went and knelt at the front of the cross," he replied.

"Yes," I said, "that was the point where I repented of everything I had done and unconditionally surrendered my life to Jesus. At that moment, I died on the cross. Jesus had asked me what I would do for him, and I had answered, 'Everything will be for you.'"

Two days after that service at church, Sarah and I were due to go to our son's school for a meeting with the headmaster. The meeting was scheduled for the morning, and so we set about getting ready nice and early. As I washed and shaved, without any warning, my back suddenly gave way in excruciating pain, and I was unable to walk. I immediately laid down on the floor at the top of the stairs, unable to move without pain shooting down my legs and up my back. This had happened to me on numerous occasions over the years. It was something that periodically hit me as a result of an injury at school when I was very young. Every now and then, my back would give out in a very painful way that would prevent me from walking and moving as normal. Each time this happened, it would usually take two to three weeks for the pain to subside and things to revert back to normal. I had been to the doctors on more than one occasion with this problem, and they had given me a series of exercises to help me recover and get back to normal.

So here I was, laying in agony at the top of the stairs.

"Do you want me to go to the school on my own and leave you here?" Sarah asked.

"No, I will get ready and come with you," I replied. "I might just be really slow because of the pain; you'll have to drive."

I slowly got up off the floor and started to get myself ready. As I got dressed, I sat on the bed to put my socks on. I was finding it very difficult to reach my feet. I sat on the bed and put my foot on some drawers so that I could lean forward to put a sock on. As I wrestled with the sock and the pain, I was taken by surprise at the words that suddenly came out of my mouth.

"This is just the devil trying to take away what God has done," I said.

This was very strange because I neither thought nor said those words, but they had come out of my mouth. I didn't understand what had just been said and had no concept of what this statement meant. However, no sooner had I said it when a burning sensation appeared at the base of my spine which quickly grew in intensity, consuming my lower back. The burning increased with a powerful sensation that drowned out the feeling of the pain. It lasted a few seconds and then began to subside. As the heat began to lift and I could feel my back again, I noticed the pain was also disappearing with it. Suddenly, I sat on the bed with no pain and was able to move in complete freedom. I thanked the Lord at what had happened and finished getting dressed.

As we headed for the door, I turned to Sarah and said, "Let's walk. I don't need to go in the car."

"What about you back?" she asked.

I replied, "God has healed it, and I am free to move. The pain has gone; let's walk down."

We left the house to walk to the school. I was completely overcome by what had just happened, and Sarah had to put up with my continued amazement and rejoicing of what had just happened as we walked to the school.

From that week onwards, I started to regularly get Bible verses coming into my head. As I started to read them, my hunger for the word of God grew. I now even started to read some of the Old Testament, whereas in the past, I had only studied the New Testament….. I had found the Old Testament too difficult to follow. I was hungry and started to understand how the word of God was like daily bread for me to feed on. I had no structured reading plan; I either read the pages where the book fell open or those verses that God gave me to study (those that came into my head). One of the early verses that came to mind was Acts 10:38:

> How God anointed Jesus of Nazareth with the Holy Spirit and power, and how he went around doing good and healing all who were under the power of the devil, because God was with him.

This was soon followed with John 14:12:

> Very truly I tell you, whoever believes in me will do the works I have been doing, and they will do even greater things than these, because I am going to the Father.

These two Bible verses spoke a lot to me from the outset. Acts 10:38 gave me an explanation about my back. This verse combined with the words that I had uttered that day made me realise that sickness was caused by the devil. He was the cause of pain and disease. This was new to me. I had never been taught this before. I didn't understand why I had been made aware of this now, other than that it helped to explain my back issues, but it would later transpire that God had some different ideas about what he was saying. The other part of this verse that made me think long and hard was the fact that Jesus had been anointed by the Holy Spirit and then healed others. For the first time, I was starting to see the importance of the Holy Spirit.

John 14:12 was a revelation too. I was seriously challenged by the fact that Jesus said we will all do the works he had been doing. I truly struggled with this concept and prayed and meditated over it for quite some time. I reflected on these Bible verses and my journey so far and, through prayer, drew a deeper understanding that we needed to be filled with the Holy Spirit and are all called to heal people and do the things that Jesus did. These Bible verses had introduced a strange and unfamiliar concept to me; I had been confronted with a new teaching. I had not heard these things taught in the sermons on Sunday mornings, and they were not something I had seen other Christians actively doing.

The whole Bible-verses-popping-in-your-head thing was quite a surprise to me. All these years that I had been going to church, I had never really read the Bible and had certainly never had Bible verses continually come to mind. Now, it didn't matter what I was doing: I could be going to bed, be washing the dinner pots, cleaning the car, or watching TV, and I would get those Bible verses in my head. Some of the verses that I received, I didn't even know if the book existed in the Bible because I hadn't heard of them before. As I received them, I wrote the verses down and then I read the Bible to see what they said.

However, I found that I now had to pray more to truly understand what this all meant. Again, over all these years of going to church, other than the prayers in church, I had never been a praying person. Now I was having to ask God to explain the Bible verses and all the things I felt he was speaking to me. As I prayed more, I was surprised to find that I was being led to answers and explanations brought about by new thoughts and further verses. This was all new, and I felt completely out of my comfort zone, but it also seemed like a newfound friendship that was exciting. I was learning how to interact with God.

Over the next few months, I lost both my uncles, with whom I had been so close. This stirred up a multitude of emotions in me over and above being struck with grief at their loss. As I remembered their kindness and all the good times with them, I was also reminded of the difficulties in my childhood. This brought me to thinking about what happens when we die; who goes to heaven, and how do we get there?

At this point in my life, I knew I had been forgiven my sins because I had accepted Jesus into my life. I was heading to heaven. But from what I knew about my uncles, I was unaware if they believed in God and unsure if they had cried out to Jesus, so I couldn't be sure if they had been saved. I felt guilty that I hadn't shared with them what had happened to me. If I had, then things might have been different and I would have known if they were in heaven. I couldn't let this happen again; my fire for Jesus was fuelled with a burning that I needed to share the good news of Jesus and his salvation message with everyone.

The death of my uncles had resurfaced emotions from my childhood; they clearly were not dealt with. Over the coming days, I wrestled with the grief and hurt at losing my uncles and the mixed-up feelings I had carried with me from my earlier years. In my prayers, I claimed the healing blood of Jesus and asked for deliverance from all my past hurts but the pain seemed to continue day after day.

Then, one day, as was usual, Sarah came home from work and I greeted her as normal. As I said hello, I started crying uncontrollably; I couldn't stop. Thinking that this was grief at the loss of my uncles, she put her arms around me to console me. After weeping for a few minutes, I then broke out into spontaneous and loud laughter, which again was uncontrollable. I laughed and laughed, and Sarah was now utterly confused….and so was I! The confusion was made worse when once again, I started to cry uncontrollably. This went on for hours. One minute, I would be weeping, and the next, I would be laughing uncontrollably. This went on for most of the day. I really felt like something was happening deep inside me. Physically, I felt like I had been on an extreme rollercoaster ride for half a day. My insides were thrown around and I felt drained.

Despite being physically wiped out by these events, strangely, I felt emotionally free. This had been a spiritual and emotional operation undertaken by Jesus. Originally, I was just as confused as my wife as to what had happened, but afterwards, when I had finally stopped, I felt like all the baggage that had weighed me down all those years had been cleared. I could feel that it was God healing me of all my past hurts. The weeping was the pain coming out, and the laughing was the joy of the Lord going in and replacing it. I now truly felt free from the burdens of the past. Also, no longer was I unsure about my identity. I knew exactly who I was: I was a child of the Father God almighty. Through the blood of Jesus Christ, I had been brought out of being an orphan and brought into sonship with the Father. My father, Abba, Daddy, God almighty. Oh, thank you, Jesus!

Now most pastors, ministers, and church Leaders would jump for joy when one of their flock experienced such a powerful series of life-changing encounters with God. Wesley certainly rejoiced on that day when I knelt down at the cross in the middle of a church service, but I observed that he seemed reserved. I wasn't sure what was going on with him, but six months after falling to my knees, I would find out.

One Friday, I called Wesley to see if I could pop round. The Lord had put it on my heart that I needed to repent of the sin in my life; I needed to do it in the presence of a witness. I didn't know why he wanted me to do it this way, but I obeyed. In Wesley's study, I knelt on the floor and repented of my sin, with him as witness to every word of repentance. As I knelt there on his study floor, I knew this was a pivotal moment in being made spotless through the blood of the Lamb. My years of stepping in and out of commitment to the Lord were done and forgotten. It was the first day of the rest of my life.

When I finished praying and got up from my knees, Wesley revealed his reservations. He knew that I had been in such a dark place and knew how fickle I had been in the previous years. Knowing this, he had waited six months to see if my repentance had been genuine and truly life changing. After seeing me on my knees in his study, he joyfully realised that God had changed me forever.

It was some weeks later, while I was still trying to make sense of everything that had been going on, that Wesley phoned to invite me to an upcoming meeting at a church in the city centre. This meeting was going to be open to all churches and an invite to hear from a missionary couple who had been in Africa for a number of years. It wasn't something I would usually go to, but as he explained all the good work they had been doing, I was compelled to say yes. Little did I know where this was going to lead!

OH MY GOSH! .....IT'S ALL REAL!

When the time came, Wesley collected me and drove us both down to the church, about twenty minutes away. It was a large building, and there were quite a lot of people there. This was the largest gathering of Christians that I had ever seen. There must have been a few hundred people, all sitting in seats facing the stage at the front. The worship struck up, and it was lively. My mind was propelled back all those years ago to the church service where I had felt very uncomfortable and now I stood there with some apprehension as to what was coming next.

As the worship continued, I didn't feel like I was part of this congregation, who were all singing their praises to Jesus. They seemed passionate and were singing their hearts out in praise, not something I felt comfortable to do in front of everyone else. I felt alienated and didn't raise my arms or sing and dance like everyone around me. I stood and watched everyone else, thinking, *Oh no, here we go again!*

Then, as I was watching, I started to hear a strange sound. It sounded something like angels singing, like a huge choir that was singing in perfect accompaniment. Looking round the room, I noticed that it wasn't a choir of angels; it was a large number of people in the room who were singing in perfect unison, in a strange way with words I couldn't understand. It seemed to be sweeping around the room like a wave going round in different directions, touching people. Even though I had been feeling really uncomfortable with what was going on, I was now drawn in to listening to this beautiful sound which was sweeping across the room. There seemed to be a heavy atmosphere developing too, which I couldn't understand; it was very real and tangible, like the air itself was getting heavy.

It took a while for the worship to conclude, and once it did, we all settled down to listen to the missionaries speak. They talked about how in faith, they had moved to Africa with no money and nowhere to live. They had started rescuing orphans from the street with no facilities or money. Over time, they had been blessed to set up numerous orphanages and churches. They had been doing great work for God. I listened in amazement at how they had been living in complete faith for all their needs. They then went on to describe all the miraculous things that they had seen God doing in Africa. They had seen people healed of lots of different illnesses, the blind getting their sight, the deaf getting their hearing, and much more. They were very humble and gave all the credit to Jesus for what had been happening.

I was mesmerised at their story and warmed to them as people who were truly doing God's work. They were deeply compassionate and humble people who I really related to. Their message presented such a challenge to me personally in the way I lived my life and also of how God is still doing miracles today. They then started to pray for people in the room, and I saw such powerful answers to prayer. I was taken back by it all. I had never seen or heard anything like this before in my life.

I really enjoyed that meeting and experienced so many new things which I didn't understand. I had so many questions and needed answers to explain these new experiences. As we left the building, I got into the Wesley's car with all these questions buzzing around in my head. He was in for a real questioning all the way home. As he turned the key to start the engine, we both turned in the car and looked at each other. Then, all of a sudden, we both burst out in uncontrollable laughter. I couldn't stop, and he couldn't stop. I laughed until my ribs were hurting, and even then, I still couldn't stop. It was as if we were intoxicated but without drinking any alcohol.

After a while, we began the ride home. This was probably the most entertaining journey I have ever experienced in a car. We continued to break out into waves of laughter. On a couple of occasions, when the laughing took a fresh hold of us, Wesley contorted with laughter, and the car weaved around on the road; he struggled to keep control, and I thought we would never get home because we would get arrested for being drunk. Fortunately, it was only a short journey home, and at the end of it we were still laughing. I knew this had been the Holy Spirit. I had read about it in the Bible, and for some strange reason, I seemed to recognise him. This had been my first taste of the Holy Spirit. I had experienced his presence and now I wanted more.

CHAPTER 9

What Could Possibly Happen Next?

Very soon after going to that church meeting and hearing from the African missionaries, I was seeking answers to all my questions. I looked in the Bible to find examples of what I had experienced, I asked Wesley for his explanation, and most importantly, I was constantly asking God what all this meant. I had experienced a lot of things which were outside my comfort zone and weren't things I had experienced in church before. I couldn't understand why I had gone to church for so long and not seen anything like this. Why was I suddenly experiencing these things now? Was it me? Was it the churches I had been attending? I needed answers; why?

One morning, I was on the train going to London for work to attend a number of meetings, and I found myself again asking God these questions and specifically what he wanted me to do. I was surprised to get an answer immediately after asking. I heard these words: "Matthew 8." I pondered for a second, thinking, *Which verses from Matthew?* However, I seemed to know which part of Matthew 8: all of it:

Jesus Heals a Man with Leprosy

When Jesus came down from the mountainside, large crowds followed him. A man with leprosy came and knelt before him and said, "Lord, if you are willing, you can make me clean."

Jesus reached out his hand and touched the man. "I am willing," he said. "Be clean!" Immediately he was cleansed of his leprosy. Then Jesus said to him, "See that you don't tell anyone. But go, show yourself to the priest and offer the gift Moses commanded, as a testimony to them."

The Faith of the Centurion

When Jesus had entered Capernaum, a centurion came to him, asking for help. "Lord," he said, "my servant lies at home paralyzed, suffering terribly."

Jesus said to him, "Shall I come and heal him?"

The centurion replied, "Lord, I do not deserve to have you come under my roof. But just say the word, and my servant will be healed. For I myself am a man under authority, with soldiers under me. I tell this one, 'Go,' and he goes; and that one, 'Come,' and he comes. I say to my servant, 'Do this,' and he does it."

When Jesus heard this, he was amazed and said to those following him, "Truly I tell you, I have not found anyone in Israel with such great faith. I say to you that many will come from the east and the west, and will take their places at the feast with Abraham, Isaac and Jacob in the kingdom of heaven. But the subjects of the kingdom will be thrown outside, into the darkness, where there will be weeping and gnashing of teeth."

Then Jesus said to the centurion, "Go! Let it be done just as you believed it would." And his servant was healed at that moment.

Jesus Heals Many

When Jesus came into Peter's house, he saw Peter's mother-in-law lying in bed with a fever. He touched her hand and the fever left her, and she got up and began to wait on him.

When evening came, many who were demon-possessed were brought to him, and he drove out the spirits with a word and healed all the sick. This was to fulfill what was spoken through the prophet Isaiah:

"He took up our infirmities
 and bore our diseases."[b]

The Cost of Following Jesus

When Jesus saw the crowd around him, he gave orders to cross to the other side of the lake. Then a teacher of the law came to him and said, "Teacher, I will follow you wherever you go."

Jesus replied, "Foxes have dens and birds have nests, but the Son of Man has no place to lay his head."

Another disciple said to him, "Lord, first let me go and bury my father."

But Jesus told him, "Follow me, and let the dead bury their own dead."

Jesus Calms the Storm

Then he got into the boat and his disciples followed him. Suddenly a furious storm came up on the lake, so that the waves swept over the But Jesus was sleeping. The disciples went and woke him, saying, "Lord, save us! We're going to drown!"

He replied, "You of little faith, why are you so afraid?" Then he got up and rebuked the winds and the waves, and it was completely calm.

The men were amazed and asked, "What kind of man is this? Even the winds and the waves obey him!"

Jesus Restores Two Demon-Possessed Men

When he arrived at the other side in the region of the Gadarenes,[c] two demon-possessed men coming from the tombs met him. They were so violent that no one could pass that way. "What do you want with us, Son of God?"

they shouted. "Have you come here to torture us before the appointed time?"

Some distance from them a large herd of pigs was feeding. The demons begged Jesus, "If you drive us out, send us into the herd of pigs."

He said to them, "Go!" So they came out and went into the pigs, and the whole herd rushed down the steep bank into the lake and died in the water. Those tending the pigs ran off, went into the town and reported all this, including what had happened to the demon-possessed men. Then the whole town went out to meet Jesus. And when they saw him, they pleaded with him to leave their region.

I sat and stared long and hard at these verses. There was a lot in them, a lot to process; what could he possibly mean? As I sat there, being rocked around as the train sped south, I asked the Lord what he meant. As I did, I was hit with what appeared to be waves of electricity going through my body. It was waves of tingling which pulsed from my head down through to my fingers and toes. As I sat there soaking up all that was happening, I heard another verse (John 14:12):

> Very truly I tell you, whoever believes in me will do the works I have been doing, and they will do even greater things than these, because I am going to the Father.

I somehow knew that the Lord wanted me to pray for the sick and see them healed and to lead others to follow him. I was still unsure what calming the storm and restoring the demon-possessed men meant, but I thought I would park that in favour of the revelation I did understand. The African missionaries had spoken about healing and salvation, not demons, so I thought it was safe to focus on healing and salvation. I said to the Lord that I would obey what he wanted me to do and asked him to show me what, when, and how. The remainder of that day went as planned, without any other encounters or peculiar events.

During the course of the following week, I continued to pray and ponder over Matthew 8. My mind kept wandering back to the church meeting with the African missionaries. They had seen a lot of these things happen and much more. It had been a revelation to hear about the life they lived. The following week, I was again called to London for further meetings. As usual, I caught the early morning train and headed into the office. After a pretty uneventful day of meetings, I headed out of the office door towards the station. It was a nice sunny day, and so I decided to walk to a different Tube station to take some air. As I walked to the station, I noticed there was a Christian bookshop on the main road. I had been wanting to get a copy of a large-print Bible for an elderly person with whom I had been sharing the gospel. I had plenty of time before the departure of my train, and so I headed into the shop to buy them one.

Once inside, I quickly found the Bible section and picked up the copy I was looking for. I started to walk to the desk to pay, but as I did, I suddenly found myself drawn from the direction of the counter and headed down the stairs. I had not planned to walk down the stairs, and I was even more surprised to suddenly find myself standing at the section of books about the Holy Spirit. I reached out and picked up a book. I was a little surprised and couldn't understand why I had just walked down the stairs and was now holding this book in my hands. By now, I was starting to get used to God's unusual ways so I decided to buy both the book and the large-print Bible.

SIMON BETHEL

Over the next few days, I found myself engrossed with the content of that book about the Holy Spirit. It talked about who the Holy Spirit was, the gifts of the Holy Spirit, and the baptism of the Holy Spirit. As I read the pages, I started to have a burning desire to be baptised in the Holy Spirit. The concept of everyone needing the baptism in the Holy Spirit was something that I hadn't previously heard about in the Sunday morning sermons. It was in the pages of this book that I learned the Biblical teaching of all believers receiving the Holy Spirit. The book had suggested that if you wanted to receive this baptism, then you should pray and ask God for it and then receive him. Over the course of the next week, I continued to pray, asking to receive the Holy Spirit, but nothing appeared to happen. Whilst praying and pondering over this lack of a response, I was drawn to Acts 8:14–17:

> When the apostles in Jerusalem heard that Samaria had accepted the word of God, they sent Peter and John to Samaria. When they arrived, they prayed for the new believers there that they might receive the Holy Spirit, because the Holy Spirit had not yet come on any of them; they had simply been baptized in the name of the Lord Jesus. Then Peter and John placed their hands on them, and they received the Holy Spirit.

Here was my answer. I needed someone to lay hands on me and pray for me to receive the Holy Spirit ... but who? I was due to go on holiday over the weekend to the Greek island of Zante, and it was now Friday; time was short. Wesley, my minister friend, was away on holiday, and so I couldn't ask him. I was completely at a loss of who I could get to lay hands on me. Then I suddenly remembered that there was a retired Anglican vicar who lived not far from me; I wondered if he would do it? I walked to his house and knocked on the door, not sure if he was at home. To my relief, he opened the door and invited me in.

I explained the events of the previous week and how I needed someone to lay hands on me so that I could receive the Holy Spirit. I never thought about it at the time, but on reflection, I wonder how most of us would react to someone knocking at our door and asking us to lay hands on them so they could receive the Holy Spirit?!

Fortunately for me, he was completely happy with my request and proceeded to lay his hands on me and pray over me. I knelt there on his lounge carpet, waiting for my Pentecost. I expected some sort of big bang, the heavens opening … something, but nothing happened, absolutely nothing as far as I could see or feel. I couldn't believe it. I got up from my knees and thanked him for the prayer and for honouring me in my request. Disheartened, I left his house, and the very next day, we went on holiday as planned.

The hotel in Zante was really nice, the weather was hot, the food was good, and we started to relax. The hotel was laid out in the shape of a U. Each side of the U contained the hotel bedrooms, and these were joined at one end by the hotel reception and restaurant. In the middle of the U was the swimming pool, which was surrounded by sun beds and parasols. At the open end of the buildings, there was a kid's play area with swings and a slide. The hotel was built at the bottom of a hill, and you walked down the drive, through reception, out of some doors, and down some steps to the pool. Each day, we would go and sit around the pool, keeping the children entertained either in the swimming pool or at the kid's play area.

One day, about halfway through the holiday, I was pushing my son, Daniel, on the swing. We were facing the pool and looking up towards reception in the distance. The weather was beautiful; it was very hot, the skies were blue, and there wasn't a cloud or a breeze in sight. People were relaxing on sun loungers around the pool which was half-full of splashing children and adults all keeping cool. The weather had been like this all holiday: wall-to-wall sunshine and heat, lovely. As I gently pushed the swing backwards and forwards, the peace and tranquillity of the place was suddenly overturned. While I gazed into the distance, a wind came from nowhere and blew over reception, across the pool, and in our direction. As it progressed across the pool area, it proceeded to blow over sun beds and parasols. In fact, the wind was so strong, it was blowing them into the pool. The best way I can describe it is that it was like a wall of wind making its way across the hotel complex.

The wind finally reached me and Daniel and blew directly at us. It was so strong that it suspended his swing in mid-air at 45 degrees and pushed me back a couple of steps until I found my balance again. All of a sudden, the wind stopped and was gone as quickly as it had arrived. Everyone was taken by surprise at the sudden appearance and disappearance of this strong wind; they were now picking up beds, umbrellas, and belongings that were strewn across the whole area.

After a short buzz and excitement of what happened, holiday mode quickly resumed. I never gave this wind a second thought and continued on with the remainder of the holiday. However, something was different, and I found that when I prayed, I now sometimes had different words coming out of my mouth which I couldn't recognize: I had started praying in tongues. On one occasion when I was praying, I saw in my mind a picture of an aeroplane on fire, and I told Sarah that there was going to be an aircraft accident. Just a couple of days later, an airplane exploded into flames in China. Fortunately, all the passengers and crew members survived, which was a relief, but I was taken aback when I saw the footage on the news; what I saw had come true. I was unsure why I had seen this picture when I had prayed a few days earlier. However, in time, I recognised that this was God teaching me how to recognise his voice and showing me how he gives us very real and practical visions so that we can do his will. This event was a way to get my attention and introduce me to how he wanted to communicate.

We returned home from holiday as planned, and it was only a few days later when my mum came to visit that the sequence of events fell into place for me. Mum had come round to hear all about our holiday and to catch up. Whilst we sat in the lounge chatting, Sarah commented on "this strange wind" that suddenly came and blew the sun beds into the pool. My mum remarked on how peculiar it was and hadn't heard of anything like it before. As she did, I suddenly realised that this was the Holy Spirit and my Pentecost.

Over the coming weeks, I learned to embrace the Holy Spirit; I learned who he was and interacted with him daily. Every day, I made it my ambition to be led by him and give him the freedom to do what he wanted. This was very difficult for those around me, as I would start to act differently and do things that didn't seem to make sense in the natural world. For example, one weekend, a friend of ours came over to visit for a few days. On the last day of their stay, they found that they had lost their house and business keys. They were due to travel home that day because they needed to get back to work, but without the keys, there would be all sorts of problems. Everyone took to looking all over the house, inside and out, to hunt down the keys. I too started to look but then paused to ask the Holy Spirit where the keys were. In the midst of everyone's anxious hunting, this appeared to be a very odd behaviour, suggesting I didn't care about finding them.

The Holy Spirit quickly showed me where they were, but there was a problem: We couldn't get to them. On the day our friend arrived, I had taken my car in for a service, and the local garage had given me a loan car. I had since collected my car and returned the loan car. The Holy Spirit showed me that the keys were on the back seat of the loan car, and because the garage was closed, they were now locked away in the workshop. I now had to convince everyone that this was where the keys were and that my friend would have to stay one extra night so that we could go and get the keys the next morning. Trying to do this based on "God telling me that's where the keys are" was very difficult, as people didn't believe me. While everyone continued to look, I sat in the confidence of knowing where the keys were. Finally, our friend agreed to stay another night so I could contact the garage the next morning. Everyone continued to ponder overnight on the location of the key, but I knew he had shown me their exact location.

Next morning, I rang the garage and explained where I thought the keys were. The service staff found them exactly where the Holy Spirit had shown me. There were many similar instances that happened many times, and people struggled to accept how I dealt with things so differently. It would take some time and a lot of other examples before people would accept that this was part of my normal life. Over time, as the evidence mounted, people began to accept that this was how the Holy Spirit worked.

Those around me were finding the change in my behaviour quite challenging. The shouting had been replaced by thoughtfulness, forgiveness, grace, and a peace that surpasses all understanding. I was disengaging from the things I used to do in order to spend more time with God and constantly listening to the Holy Spirit. Whereas I used to watch lots of TV and films, I now wanted to be doing things for the Lord instead. Watching TV had always been a real family event in our house. People couldn't understand why I now spent very little time watching it.

There was a good reason why I had disengaged from the television. One evening, when I was sat in the lounge with my wife watching a programme, Jesus appeared in the corner of the room and asked me why I was watching TV when he was so desperate to spend time with me. Then, all of a sudden, I had a vision where I stood next to Jesus, and we were in someone else's lounge. There were people watching TV and Jesus was saying, "I am over here; come and spend time with me." His voice was full of longing and passion to spend time with people, and he had his arms stretched out towards them, willing them to come to him. However, they never even looked up and just continued to watch TV. We flashed through a number of different lounges with different people watching TV and Jesus calling out to them, but none replied. All of a sudden, I was back in my lounge, and all I could see was the look of longing on Jesus's face. He was desperate to spend time with people he loved. This challenged me to spend less time in front of the TV and more time in his presence.

Around this time, the Holy Spirit took me on a journey of new verses in the Bible. There were a few Bible verses that became imprinted on my heart and burnt into my mind. One particularly powerful verse was Romans 12:2:

> Do not conform to the pattern of this world, but be transformed by the renewing of your mind.

I started to seek more revelation by spending more time with God and reading his word in order that my mind would continue to be transformed. I looked out for those worldly things that were a distraction and chose to remove myself from anything that appeared unholy, not aligned to God's will, or a diversion from doing his work. This was a big change in me, and those around me found it very difficult to comprehend. Some of our close friends we regularly went out with withdrew from engaging with us, and our social life started to disappear. I wouldn't sit in front of the TV anymore but would praise, worship, pray, and read instead.

Sarah was concerned about my behaviour. She had seen me focus on the business all those years ago; she had seen me focus on my career and become materialistic. She was now seeing me completely changing direction again. I can understand why she found this difficult; it had all the warning signs of another one of my disasters looming, but this time, I was changing for the better, and it was being orchestrated by God.

Someone at the time commented to me, "It's all or nothing with you, isn't it?"

I replied, "I have always been tenacious but just never had the correct purpose; now I do."

I was becoming humbled before the Lord. I was no longer materialistic. I no longer wanted fame and fortune; I just wanted to honour God and do my part in seeing Jesus glorified throughout the world. Whereas before I had a big ego, I now wanted people to look straight through me and remember Jesus, not Simon. Previously, I had been out for self-gain and success; now, I was full of compassion for the lost and needy. I had experienced the powerful grace and mercy of Jesus Christ, and he was now my passion.

These were all very big changes, indeed. I felt that I was living at odds with those I loved and couldn't seem to be able to clearly articulate what I was going through. While they had their own concerns, this was no walk in the park for me, either. I had my own struggles going through all of this change, but everyone around me seemed to ignore this. I was torn between what Jesus wanted and what everyone else I loved thought was normal. There was a big gap between the two, and I was stuck in the middle, but this seemed to go unnoticed. They had known me a long time and seen me go through many changes, so I guessed that to them, this had all the warning signs of another one of those changes. It probably brought back their fears of how I had responded to previous changes in my life, how it always came with some sort of disaster and an impact to those around me. These were difficult times indeed, and I was starting to feel like the world was against me. I felt I was living the life that Jesus had described in Luke 12:51–52:

> Do you think I came to bring peace on earth? No, I tell you, but division. From now on there will be five in one family divided against each other, three against two and two against three.

I was humbled, ready for action; what was next?

CHAPTER 10

Hang on Tight and Ride that Bull; God Is on It with You Too

Things had started to change at church. The services still had quite a structure around them, but the worship was starting to become more vibrant and last longer. I was starting to really feel the presence of God during these periods of freer worship. The irony of it; whereas previously, I would have been uncomfortable with this type of worship, now I yearned to worship God freely and in any way that the Holy Spirit directed me to do so. My eyes were no longer on me and how I might look to other people; my focus and heart were now on Jesus. I no longer cared what worship looked like; I just wanted to exalt him and encounter God. The main thing for me was to glorify him in truth and encounter him in a way that would continue to change me for his glory. I was less interested in the content and structure of worship and more interested in being led into his presence and an encounter.

Another one of the changes at church was the appearance of a ministry team, of which I was a member. The ministry team were there to pray for people when requested, which could be at various times throughout the service. Somewhere during the service, an announcement would made that the ministry team were in the corner of the room, and if anyone would like prayer for anything, they could go over to the team. This was a relatively new thing and had been part of the service for only a short few months. One particular day, it was my turn to be on the ministry team. As was common, there were two of us scheduled to pray for people that day. It was a typical service, nothing special organised, and towards the end, the announcement was given that prayer ministry was available. As people sang another worship song, a husband and wife came forward, and the wife requested that we pray over her. She closed her eyes, and as I would normally do, I placed my hand on the wife's shoulder while her husband had his arm around her, and I started to pray. After a few minutes of prayer, I stepped back so that they could go back to their seats. However, upon stepping back, there seemed to be something wrong. The wife appeared to be unable to stand up; her eyes were still closed. Her legs had buckled beneath her and were like jelly.

"Let's gently lay her on the floor," I said.

The husband replied, "Great, I was struggling to hold her up. I have been supporting her for the last couple of minutes."

I was really surprised at his statement, as I had been unaware of anything happening.

We gently laid her down on the floor and continued to pray over her. I wasn't sure what had happened; I had never seen this before.

"God is touching her," the lady who was praying with me whispered.

Fortunately for me, she had seen this many times before in other places of ministry. I, on the other hand, had never experienced this before and was a little shocked at seeing this happen. I wasn't the only one; there was a mixed reaction across the church. Amongst the church congregation, there were people who knew that God was doing something. But on the flip side, there were those who didn't understand what was happening and were wanting to medically assist the wife, thinking she had passed out. A small commotion was building up. Some people wanted to call for the paramedics, whilst others tried to reassure them it was God doing his work. Fortunately, very soon after being laid on the floor, the wife stood up to declare that Jesus had been ministering to her.

This was the first time that I had seen this happen. I had a lot of questions. Why did God make her fall on the floor? What was he doing? Why hadn't I been aware of what was happening? I searched my Bible and prayed to try and understand what had just happened and how God worked like this. Over the next few weeks, I learned much more about how God's touch can be overpowering, causing people to fall over under his power. As well as my Bible and prayer revelations, there were a number of people in the church who recognised what God had been doing, and I was able to discuss this with them. Wesley also started to teach the church on the subject. John 18:5–6:

> "I am he," Jesus said. (And Judas the traitor was standing there with them.) When Jesus said, "I am he," they drew back and fell to the ground.

I understood that the wife had encountered Jesus, and as he had approached her, she had fallen to the ground.

Over the coming weeks, people rejoiced about what God had started to do, but unfortunately, some people were uncomfortable with what had happened. I found myself becoming the subject of a small amount of criticism over something God did. Each time someone challenged me over the events that had occurred, the Lord gave me the words to respond.

When confronted about it, my reply would be, "Let me ask you a question. Do you think that I woke up that Sunday morning deciding that I was going to make someone fall on the floor in church? I mean, even if I had, there is no possible way that I could have made it happen; I am not a hypnotist or a magician. Neither could I have pushed the wife over because her husband was holding her, and I had stepped back. Even the wife said this was Jesus ministering to her. There is no conceivable way that I could have thought this up and then come up with a plan and execute it. Also, to what purpose could I have done this? What would I gain from making someone fall on the floor? Do you think I caused this?"

After consideration, the answer was reluctantly given: *no*. This was of God; I knew it, and I wasn't going to even dare challenge him on it. If he wanted to work like that, it was okay with me. I was finding that following Jesus in truth was not a simple walk in the park.

It was only a few weeks after this occurrence that I had my own experience of God's overpowering presence. It was a Sunday morning service, and towards the end, Wesley made an appeal for a response to anyone who was hungry for God to go to the front and receive prayer and a blessing. I knew I was hungry and made my way to the front. Standing there at the front of the church, someone from the ministry team came over and started to pray over me. As they did, I started to be overcome by a very heavy presence around me. It was similar to the vortex of peace that I had been in all those years ago, but this time, it was accompanied by a weightiness. The air around me got heavier, and very soon afterwards, I was pressed to the floor, face up, laying on my back. I couldn't get up, and my eyes were closed.

All of a sudden, I had a picture of Jesus riding towards me on a white horse. He rode up to me and dismounted. Even though I was physically pressed to the floor on my back, in the picture, I stood before Jesus. He came to me and put a red robe over me, and he fastened it around my neck, saying, "This is yours; you dropped it, but now I am putting it back on you." He then mounted his horse and rode away.

As he rode away, the picture faded, and the heavy presence started to lift, allowing me to get up from the floor. I was now asking Jesus if the dream was real; had I just imagined it? Could he give me confirmation? What did it mean? As I stood there, a woman who had been seated in the congregation and not been involved approached me and put her hand on my shoulder.

She looked me squarely in the eyes and said, "I sat over the other side of the church, and when you fell to the ground, I had a vision. In the vision, I saw Jesus putting a red cape around your neck."

That was my confirmation. I was in awe that God had not only given me the encounter but had provided me with confirmation through a long-standing Christian I respected.

Over the years, I have come to understand that people have different reactions to events such as these. Some people embrace all too easily everything that has happened without a sound discernment if it was something of God; they place themselves at risk of falling into error unless they listen to God continually. Others can be overly cautious in their concern to not be deceived by falsehood. They can be at risk of denying a genuine act of God because they have a lack of discernment over what is happening.

I understand the reasons why people might have either of these reactions. Sadly, it is possible for people to pretend or overstate that God is at work for their own personal gain, and therefore, it is important that we have spiritual discernment to understand when the Lord is truly working verses when something is not of God. I have come to realise that we need to listen closely to God and not block out his voice by being too cynical, dismissing every true work of God just because there are instances of falsehood or things we simply don't understand.

For example, one evening, we held a worship meeting to exalt God. We sang and worshipped for about an hour and then left space for God to share a word and minister to people. As we prayed over people, one lady fell to the floor, appearing to be having an encounter with the Lord.

All of a sudden, the Holy Spirit said to me, "This is not of God."

I knelt down, put my hand on her shoulder, and whispered, "Let her have a true encounter with you, Jesus. Let this be of you, Lord."

The moment I stopped speaking, she inhaled deeply, stared wide-eyed at me, and then started to weep; now she was having a genuine encounter with the Lord.

There are many people who are fearful of such things, like seeing someone being touched by God and falling down. In their fear, they reject that these things are of God. There can be numerous reasons why they are uncomfortable; maybe they themselves aren't filled with the Holy Spirit and don't recognise that it is God doing something. Maybe they have previously been hurt by something not genuinely of God. Or it could be that they are uncomfortable with such events because they have never been taught about it or seen God working in this way. I can relate with those people. I know how they feel because I used to feel the same way when I experienced anything that was different and deviated from the normality of my structured Sunday morning service.

Over time, I too had to learn that God does work in different ways and ways that we might not understand. When God does something different and we see people who are unsure of what is happening, it is important that we help them to recognise him and overcome their fears by explaining that this is one of the ways in which God works. Our explanation needs to be combined with a sound Biblical teaching that explains what is happening. If someone had done that with me all those years ago, I would probably have learned to embrace what God was doing much sooner.

The experience of seeing encounters with Jesus in such powerful ways started to really open my eyes to the fact that he works in a spiritual and supernatural way. It brought back to mind my own previous encounters and how he had been so practical in my life. I was on a journey, seeing the Lord do more and more but struggling with the mere concept of how he worked and that he required us to be actively involved. He was working in natural, spiritual, and supernatural ways that were contrary to my logical brain. It was clear that I needed to knock down some of the roadblocks that existed in my mind, which had been put there over all the years of my own life experiences and the teaching of those around me. This was to become a real battleground in my mind, but I was desperate and hungry to see the truth and rawness of God (not the refined boxed-up version that I had previously controlled). Through scripture, prayer, and these new experiences, God started to transform me through the renewing of my mind. Romans 12:2:

> Do not conform to the pattern of this world, but be transformed by the renewing of your mind.

Not long after these events, I had to go to London for two days of meetings in my job. This visit required an overnight stay in a hotel in the city centre. As was usual for me, I travelled down to London on the train and then had a full day of meetings in the office. After the meetings had concluded for the first day, I retired to the hotel to have some dinner and an early night (this was a stark contrast to the evenings of socialising I used to do when away). After a good night's sleep, I awoke early to the sound of bins being collected outside on the streets and the noise of early-morning traffic passing my London hotel.

Laying there awake in bed, a very strange thing happened: I suddenly found that I was standing before God. He was there, right before my very eyes. I no longer saw the hotel room but was in a glass building. God started to head off into other glass rooms, and I walked alongside him, listening to what he said. We walked around a series of glass rooms, and all the time, he talked to me about the things that had been going on in my life. He also talked to me about some other Bible verses from Revelation, answering some of my burning questions. It was all very powerful.

He then said something that really hit me: "Simon, all you need to know can be found in the book of Daniel. It will give you answers to your questions."

The words seemed to sink into the inside of me. It was surreal; here I was walking with God, clearly hearing all that he said, but at the same time, in the distance, I could make out the noise of the bins and the traffic outside the hotel. As soon as he finished speaking, I found myself back in the hotel room, accompanied only by the sound of the clattering bins and cars on the road. However, the words God had spoken were alive inside me. I was hungry to read the book of Daniel.

This was an Old Testament book that I had never read or even opened, but over the course of the next few days, I read and reread its contents. The book of Daniel spoke to me on many fronts, and there was one verse that spoke directly into what had recently happened in church. Daniel 8:17–18 spoke of falling prostrate in an encounter, similar to what had happened:

> As he came near the place where I was standing, I was terrified and fell prostrate. "Son of man,"[b] he said to me, "understand that the vision concerns the time of the end."
>
> While he was speaking to me, I was in a deep sleep, with my face to the ground. Then he touched me and raised me to my feet.

There were many things that I drew from the book of Daniel which were relevant to this particular period in my life. I also drew some key messages that would establish some cornerstones to my faith. One of the key messages that penetrated deep was about how Daniel trusted God in everything; he was unwavering in his worship and resolute in following God's ways, even when those around him conspired to destroy him. He loved God, encountered God, and refused to step away from the path of the truth. This was the approach I was to take. God had shown me to be like Daniel, and trusting God with all he was showing me and to be unwavering when those around me tried to get me to change course; my mind was being further renewed.

Another key lesson I took from the book of Daniel was how he was constantly on his knees in prayer and worship, even when there was a decree banning such practice. He had a trust in God that came from praying and being in his presence. It was a trust that came from an intimate relationship and produced an unwavering faith. This was the type of relationship that I was developing with the Lord. Daniel 6:10–22:

OH MY GOSH! .....IT'S ALL REAL!

Now when Daniel learned that the decree had been published, he went home to his upstairs room where the windows opened toward Jerusalem. Three times a day he got down on his knees and prayed, giving thanks to his God, just as he had done before. Then these men went as a group and found Daniel praying and asking God for help. So they went to the king and spoke to him about his royal decree: "Did you not publish a decree that during the next thirty days anyone who prays to any god or human being except to you, Your Majesty, would be thrown into the lions' den?"

The king answered, "The decree stands—in accordance with the law of the Medes and Persians, which cannot be repealed."

Then they said to the king, "Daniel, who is one of the exiles from Judah, pays no attention to you, Your Majesty, or to the decree you put in writing. He still prays three times a day." When the king heard this, he was greatly distressed; he was determined to rescue Daniel and made every effort until sundown to save him.

Then the men went as a group to King Darius and said to him, "Remember, Your Majesty, that according to the law of the Medes and Persians no decree or edict that the king issues can be changed."

So the king gave the order, and they brought Daniel and threw him into the lions' den. The king said to Daniel, "May your God, whom you serve continually, rescue you!"

> A stone was brought and placed over the mouth of the den, and the king sealed it with his own signet ring and with the rings of his nobles, so that Daniel's situation might not be changed. Then the king returned to his palace and spent the night without eating and without any entertainment being brought to him. And he could not sleep.
>
> At the first light of dawn, the king got up and hurried to the lions' den. When he came near the den, he called to Daniel in an anguished voice, "Daniel, servant of the living God, has your God, whom you serve continually, been able to rescue you from the lions?"
>
> Daniel answered, "May the king live forever! My God sent his angel, and he shut the mouths of the lions. They have not hurt me, because I was found innocent in his sight. Nor have I ever done any wrong before you, Your Majesty."

I could see it now: Daniel had intimacy, faith, and honour, and as a result, he saw God do supernatural things for him because of their relationship. It was from intimacy that Daniel did everything for God. Intimacy was to become my focus: to be a friend with God and to understand what he wanted me to do. As I spent more time with the Lord, he gave me other Bible verses that would further convince me that he had a plan for my life and wanted me to work with him. There were also verses that reaffirmed that all the things Jesus said were for us today just as much as they were for the apostles.

Two of these verses were Acts 6:8 and Acts 10:37–38, which became two more key cornerstones on which I would further build my faith.

Acts 10:37–38 was a real eye opener. It clearly showed that the devil was the cause of illness:

> You know what has happened throughout the province of Judea, beginning in Galilee after the baptism that John preached—how God anointed Jesus of Nazareth with the Holy Spirit and power, and how he went around doing good and healing all who were under the power of the devil, because God was with him.

So the cause of all sickness was the devil, and we are to be like Jesus, doing good and healing them, because God was with us; again, this comes from intimacy. As well as showing me that it was the devil who caused illness, I drew two other key learnings from this verse: Firstly, Jesus needed to be anointed with the Holy Spirit in order to heal the sick, and secondly, his intent clearly was to heal the sick, setting them free from the power of the devil. His intent was not to see people ill. This was such a simple but powerful revelation to me.

In Acts 6, I read about Steven, who was picked to undertake the menial task of serving tables. I read how his combination of being filled with the Holy Spirit and having a great faith (similar to Daniel) allowed him to perform many powerful acts, similar to Jesus. This was one of a number of examples in the New Testament where others did the same works as Jesus: miracles, signs, and wonders. My mind needed to be renewed in the revelation that we are all called to do these works, just as much as the apostles. Acts 6:5–8:

> They chose Stephen, a man full of faith and of the Holy Spirit; also Philip, Procorus, Nicanor, Timon, Parmenas, and Nicolas from Antioch, a convert to Judaism. They presented these men to the apostles, who prayed and laid their hands on them.
>
> So the word of God spread. The number of disciples in Jerusalem increased rapidly, and a large number of priests became obedient to the faith.
>
> Now Stephen, a man full of God's grace and power, performed great wonders and signs among the people.

The combination of being filled with the Holy Spirit and having a real, unmovable faith was a key principle that God was teaching me. As well as being filled with the Holy Spirit, he was showing me I needed to have an unwavering faith that was borne out of intimacy with him. This would allow me to be led by God and also effective in my co-labouring with him. The Lord was showing me that today, we need to have faith for the miraculous because it is his intent to see people healed and set free from the power of the devil.

To reaffirm this message, the Lord gave me another verse: Luke 10:1–3, 8–9, 17, where Jesus sent out seventy-two people, commanding them to heal the sick:

Jesus Sends Out the Seventy-Two

> After this the Lord appointed seventy-two[a] others and sent them two by two ahead of him to every town and place where he was about to go. He told them, "The

harvest is plentiful, but the workers are few. Ask the Lord of the harvest, therefore, to send out workers into his harvest field. Go! I am sending you out like lambs among wolves. … When you enter a town and are welcomed, eat what is offered to you. Heal the sick who are there and tell them, 'The kingdom of God has come near to you.'" … The seventy-two returned with joy and said, "Lord, even the demons submit to us in your name."

Repeatedly, I learned that it wasn't just Jesus who was anointed to do the work, but others were also anointed and commissioned in his name. My renewed mind was settling in to the truth of John 14:12. The Lord was changing my perspective so I could understand that I needed to bear fruit for him and that I needed to be effective in my work with him out in the harvest fields. He constantly reminded me of Matthew 8. As this revelation of co-labouring with the Lord increased, the fire inside me increased. I started to feel like I would burst. Every time I saw someone who was sick or in need, I had to share the gospel and pray over them. I found I was consumed by this passion that was welling up inside me. I went in hot pursuit of the lost and the sick, looking to share the good news of Jesus and pray for all who were sick so that they could be healed.

I prayed for a whole year and saw nothing in return. Not one healing and not one person saved in the name of Jesus. As the year progressed, I started to have doubts if I had read God correctly. Was I wrong? Should I be doing this? My doubt was compounded by people starting to question if I should be pursuing praying for healing as much as I was. There was little evidence of any healings, and it seemed a difficult walk. However, as I spent time with God, I was constantly reminded of those Bible verses, and so the battle persisted. The only answer I could see was to seek God even more, like Daniel had. Unknown to me, I was learning a valuable lesson. I was learning that I had to spend more time with God. I needed to be in his presence in order to get closer to him and then go out and to do his works in his strength and not my own. I was learning not to rely on myself but to be wholly dependent on his Holy Spirit. I continued to soak up more and more of his presence, spending time with him.

As the weeks passed by, I began to see people being healed by the Lord. I started to see him reveal himself to others, and they would come to faith in Jesus. It was a gradual thing, like a tap being turned on. The more time I spent with God and believed his word, the more I humbled myself and pursued an increased holiness and righteousness in my life. As I pursued him more, I started to be more separated from the ways of the world. The more I turned my attention to God and not worldly things, the more I saw Jesus at work; this was a simple but powerful truth. As time progressed, I started to see him do increasingly powerful things.

As my wife and I both worked, time was short, and we needed help getting some of the household chores done, so a cleaner was employed to come to the house every Friday morning. For a number of years, my job had allowed me to work from home most Fridays, which meant that we started to get to know each other quite well; over the years, she become a good family friend. It was on one Friday when she came to clean as normal that things were taken to a whole new level. About three-quarters of the way through cleaning the house, she started to complain of pain in her fingers, and so I asked what was wrong.

"It's my arthritis," she explained. "It has got so bad that I can't do certain things anymore … things such as opening the tops of jars.

In fact, my friend has bought me a device to help me to open jars. I can't open them like I used to be able to, when I grip them and twist, I can't turn the lid because the pain is that bad."

I was overcome by a sense that God wanted to do something. I took a jar out of the fridge and handed it to her. "Show me," I said.

She took the jar from me and attempted to open it but couldn't because of the pain. She gave the jar back to me, and then what happened next took me as much by surprise as it did her.

"Watch this," I said. It was one of those times when words popped out of my mouth, but I hadn't said them.

"Watch what?" she asked with a quizzical look on her face.

"Wait here a minute," I replied. I walked into another room and prayed, "Lord, you said those words from my mouth, not me. Therefore, it's all up to you and not down to me. I give this all to you." I returned to stand in front of her.

"Give me your hands," I said, and taking her hands, I continued, "I command the pain to go in the name of Jesus. I command the arthritis to leave in the name of Jesus, and I speak health, strength, and pain-free movement over your fingers and hands in the name of Jesus. Thank you, Father."

I took the jar again and tightened the lid nice and tight, then I gave it to her, saying, "Try now."

She took the jar and, because she had seen me tighten it, braced herself. She screwed up her face as she prepared for the searing pain and then twisted her hands. The lid popped off the jar. The expression on her face changed from a grimace to a complete look of shock.

She exclaimed, "The pain – it's … it's gone!" She kept tightening and taking off the jar lid in utter amazement and joy. Each time she did so, her mouth dropped open wider and wider, compounding the look of shock on her face.

I thanked the Lord and explained that Jesus had done this because he loved her and cared about her. I asked her if she would like to know Jesus as her Lord and Saviour. She replied yes, and so I led her in a prayer, asking Jesus to be her Lord and Saviour. The fire of God's touch descended through her body, and she then collapsed on the couch in his presence. She was bright red at the fire of his touch and stayed there for some time as Jesus ministered to her.

Another time, Sarah's hairdresser (Mia) was coming to our house to cut her hair. Shortly before the appointment, Mia called ahead to ask if someone would be able to take her to the hospital, as her four-year-old daughter had been admitted quite ill. The doctors had found shadows on her lungs, and she was laid on a hospital bed, very weak. I said I would take her. Sarah agreed, as she knew that if the chance presented itself, I would go to pray for Mia's daughter. Interestingly, my daughter at this time had started to see all the things that God was doing and asked if she could come along too; she had an expectation that something good was going to happen. Mia was not a Christian and so during the journey to the hospital, I explained what had been happening and how Jesus was healing people. She was amazed at what had been happening. I asked her if she would like me to come in and pray for her daughter to be healed. She agreed. As we drove to the hospital and chatted, a very heavy presence of God developed. The air got heavy, and the temperature got warmer and warmer, as if there was a fire in the air. Mia could feel the heat; it was getting very hot. She looked like she had been under a sunlamp; her face and neck were glowing red. I glanced through the mirror into the back seat, and Alex was also looking quite red in the face. We were all overcome by the atmosphere and the tangible presence of the Lord.

When we arrived at the hospital, it wasn't visiting hours, so the hospital was reasonably quiet. It also meant that I shouldn't be in the hospital at this time. We walked the corridors and took the lift to get to the ward. As we entered, I was struck by how quiet the ward was; everything we said or did could be heard. We approached the bed where Mia's daughter was laying. In the quiet, I drew the curtains around the bed and started to pray over her, declaring healing in the name of Jesus and telling the illness to leave in the name of Jesus. After a short time praying, the curtains parted, and a nurse stepped in.

"What's going on here?" she asked; it was obvious that I shouldn't have been there.

"He just came here to pray over my daughter," Mia replied.

I interjected before the nurse could reply, "We have finished now and will leave." I nodded at Alex for us to leave and looked at Mia and her daughter, saying, "Goodbye, see you later."

All of a sudden, we were completely surprised to see the young girl sit bolt upright in bed and say, "See you, thanks for coming."

I will never forget the look on the nurse's face that night, such surprise to see the sudden change in the daughter's responsiveness. Within two days, the daughter had been released from hospital. Shortly after, I had a further conversation with Mia.

She said, "I have to take my daughter to the hospital for another scan to see what has happened to those shadows on her lungs."

I replied, "They are gone; her lungs are clean. Jesus has taken it all away; they will not find anything, no shadows, nothing."

"We'll see," was her response.

Shortly after the hospital appointment, Mia again came to our house. I will always remember the look of amazement on her face as she explained that the hospital hadn't found anything. Her lungs were clear. Thank you, Jesus.

These were all great testimonies of what Jesus was doing, and I loved co-labouring with him. People were desperate and in need, and the answer was Jesus. However, despite the joy of seeing what he was doing, there was the pain that came from seeing the continued despair of those who were not healed. I couldn't understand it. There wasn't a formula. I just expected everyone to be healed and didn't compute why some weren't. However, the fact that some were not healed and the fact that I had no answer why did not seem like any reason for me to stop praying for the sick. Whatever was wrong was obviously something wrong with me and not with God. Some people took great pleasure in pointing out that not everyone was healed. These were Christian people who took delight in seeing me fail and trying to undermine what God had been teaching me. I continued to listen to the Lord and continued to pray, and some were healed, and some were not. There didn't seem to be any rhyme or reason to it.

One day, I was walking home from church with my son and a lady from the congregation. She started to tell me about her arthritis, which was starting to affect the things she liked to do.

In the middle of the street, I took her hands and simply said, "I command the arthritis and pain to get out in the name of Jesus."

It took a few seconds, and the Lord healed her of her pain. A few weeks later, I was talking to someone in church who had been suffering with back pain for months.

I prayed for her, and she simply looked at me and said, "Thank you, but it is still there," and walked away. I was confused. Two hours later, I bumped into her near the church; she had been trying to find me because the pain had left, and she could move freely. Not long after that, I prayed for someone's ankle; they were in pain and needed an operation. When I had finished praying, I looked up with an expectation of them being healing. There was nothing. No healing, nothing. I couldn't understand any of it. All I knew was that I had to keep doing the Lord's work. It was worth it for every person the Lord healed.

By now, I had seen the Lord heal people, and I had seen people give their lives to Jesus. Matthew 8 was starting to be a reality. However, what about the rest of Matthew 8? There was more than just healing in Matthew 8. The Lord had been clear in showing me that all of it applied…….. things were going to get even crazier.

CHAPTER 11

Things Just Get Crazier, but It appears to be God's Normal

These had been very exciting times seeing the Lord do all these things: healing people, ministering deeply to others, and then seeing them come into a relationship with Jesus as they accepted him as Lord and Saviour. It had also been a tough time seeing prayers going unanswered and some people not getting healed. I didn't understand why people weren't healed, but I knew that I had to continue pressing forward doing the things that God had asked me to do. As I wrestled with the fact that some people were not being healed, I realised that the failings were with me and not God. I accepted that I would never be able to explain why some weren't healed; this was because of my own imperfections, which would always remain while I am on this earth. It was something that I would have to continue to work through and God was going to inspire me by giving me a glimpse of something greater.

Life was certainly busy; my job was demanding, time with the family was important, and so too was the Lord's work. People at church would say to me, "You need to slow down, you do too much," and I would reply, "Yes, but it is a matter of life and death ... literally."

I had reasoned that in the New Testament, the Holy Spirit had quickened Paul physically to enable him to walk thousands of miles to share the gospel. He had been sustained by God, and I thought that if it was good enough for him, then I could experience the same. My motivation was to see people come to know the truth and for them to be taken into a deep relationship with Jesus, confident of their eternal salvation. I had a fire in me to see the hurting restored and healed. I had a fire for people to become aware of the reality of the Holy Spirit and be baptised and anointed. No selfish motivations, no desire for recognition; I just wanted people to know Jesus.

Someone once said to me, "I don't know how you can walk up to a complete stranger in the street and offer to pray for them; I would feel embarrassed to do that."

I replied, "When I do that, my eyes are not on myself but on the needs of the individual in front of me. If I am looking at myself, then I become overly self-conscious. Keeping my eyes on the one in front of me means I have no concept of how I look. I just try to look at the person before me in love and through Jesus's eyes. We need to take our eyes off ourselves and turn them to others."

I had learned to see people through the eyes of love. I read in the Bible how Jesus often looked on people with compassion, and I was feeling something similar. I had taken my eyes off me and put them on others with kindness and love.

I truly had a passion for the lost (those not yet saved through a living relationship with Jesus); amongst other activities to satisfy this hunger, I started to do some street work with various members from our church. We would arrange events so we could just pour love on the local community and spread the good news of Jesus. This would take many forms: serving drinks and biscuits, setting up prayer tents, and just walking the streets to see what the Holy Spirit told us to do. I was hungry to fulfil what God had called me to do. Since the day he put Matthew 8 in my mind, I had seen parts of it come to pass. I had seen the Lord heal people. I had seen people give their lives to Jesus. Matthew 8 was starting to become a reality. However, what about the rest of Matthew 8? The Lord had shown me all of it applied, but as of yet, there was so much I hadn't experienced. Things were going to get even crazier.

It was during the planning of one of these events that the kingdom of heaven started to come nearer. We were planning an evening outreach to the local youth. The plan was that we organise a small activity just outside the church building. This would consist of setting up a gazebo and table, and then serving drinks and biscuits to passers-by. We were emailing backwards and forwards trying to agree on a date to do this when all of a sudden, one Thursday morning, the Lord spoke to me and said that we needed to do it that very evening. As the morning progressed, another person from church emailed me to say the Lord had spoken to her and said we needed to do the outreach that same evening. I took this as confirmation that we should quickly arrange with others to go out later that day.

However, there was a problem. There was a meeting scheduled at church for the same time, which meant that some people would not be available. Everyone encouraged the two of us to come up with an alternative date. There was a flurry of emails, and amongst it all, we explained that the Lord had spoken to us individually, saying that we should do the outreach that evening. After some negotiation, church leaders reluctantly cancelled in favour of undertaking the outreach.

A group of us converged on the church at six o'clock, ready to serve refreshments to the local community as they passed by. However, there was now another problem: It was pouring with torrential rain and had been all afternoon. I started to question whether I had heard the Lord clearly. People would not be happy after all the hassle of rearranging that meeting if we couldn't get outside. We met in the church hall to pray for the upcoming events. While we prayed, I was convicted by the Holy Spirit to take authority over the rain and commanded the rain to stop and the sun to come out in the name of Jesus. It was a real conviction and not something I had ever done before. It felt like something rising from deep inside me.

Once again, I found myself really bowing to the leading of the Holy Spirit. After we finished praying, the rain subsided, and the sunshine came out, so we proceeded to set up the gazebo, table and refreshments outside. Once everything was ready, we stood and waited for the passers-by. We waited and waited, but there was yet another problem: Due to the heavy rain, it appeared that everyone had stayed indoors; there were no passers-by. The two of us who had been impressed by the Lord to do the outreach that evening decided that we would go for a walk into the nearby park to find some people we could invite back to the gazebo. As we walked through the park's trees, we were suddenly powerfully overcome by the Holy Spirit and began to laugh uncontrollably. As we walked on, our laughter and erratic behaviour attracted the attention of three young men, who wondered what we were doing. Amidst all the laughing, we managed to invite them for a hot chocolate, to which they said yes.

Back at the gazebo, I chatted to one of the young men about how we were from the local church and just extending our love to the community by serving refreshments. He said he didn't believe in God and told me he was just about to join the army. As we chatted, I steered the conversation towards what he thought might happen to him when he died.

SIMON BETHEL

"I am not sure," he replied. "I guess there is nothing once you die."

"I used to believe there was nothing," I continued, "until I encountered Jesus and found out that he was the only way to get to heaven. Would you like to accept Jesus into your life and know that if anything was to happen to you, you would get into heaven ... remove the risk you might not get in?"

"I guess so," he answered. "I would like to think I would get into heaven."

I placed my hand on his shoulder and led him in a prayer to repent of his sins and accept Jesus as his Lord and Saviour. At the end of the prayer, I asked the Holy Spirit to enter him and fill him with the presence of the Lord. No sooner had I finished speaking, when he suddenly fell to the ground and laid in the wet grass. I continue to pray over him while he was on the ground, and then suddenly, after a couple of minutes, he jumped to his feet.

He had a look of surprise on his face; he grabbed me by the shoulders and said, with wide eyes, "I just got Jesus. Jesus is real."

"I know," I replied.

"No ... no ... Jesus is real," he exclaimed, eyes wide open. "I just met him."

"I know," I repeated, laughing.

As the rain had stopped some time ago, people had started to appear. The young man suddenly ran towards an approaching group of teenage boys. They instantly recognised him; he was known to the local youth as a real troublemaker, and now he was running at them. He could be about to do anything to them. As he ran at the group, they braced themselves for what was coming, expecting the worst.

He suddenly stopped and leant forward, saying, "Jesus is real. You need to listen to these guys, who can tell you about him."

They were utterly shocked at what he had said, and so I explained to them what had just happened, and we all ended up praying together. This happened a number of times that evening before we finally packed up and headed to our homes. We had swapped contact details with the young men in order to stay in touch and help them with their walk with the Lord.

We were all in awe of what Jesus had been doing that evening, how he had orchestrated us to go out on the street that particular night and then to see him at work in such a powerful way. There had been salvations and healings. It was all in God's timing because the following week, the boys were due to join the army, facing the reality that they would soon be heading out to the conflict in the Middle East. If we had waited another week, we would have missed it. God is on the lookout for obedient people who will listen and follow what he instructs them to do. We just need to spend time with him to listen and then be obedient.

As we packed up, Wesley made me laugh with a comment he made. He said, "Can you imagine what this might have looked like to someone who was walking past and not plugged into what was going on? One minute, I saw you talking to a young lad who was getting animated and shouting. You reached out and put your hand on his shoulder, and then I briefly looked away because someone asked me something. As I turned back round to look at you, I saw the young lad was laid out on the wet grass, motionless! What would that have looked like to a passer-by?"

I laughed as I thought about it.

When I got home, I praised God for all that he had done that evening. He had asked us to go out that particular night and honoured us with a change in the weather that allowed us to see people come to faith in Jesus Christ. The Holy Spirit had moved powerfully that

SIMON BETHEL

evening. This was church; this was the life of the Christian as God designed it to be. As I prepared to go to bed, my phone rang, and I answered it.

"Is this Simon Bethel?" a strange voice asked.

"Yes, it is," I replied. "Who is this, and how can I help?"

"Did you meet a young man tonight?" a woman's voice asked directly. "Did you pray for him?"

I answered, "Yes, I did, who is this please?"

She replied, "I am his mother, and I can't believe the difference in my son since he came home tonight. He has really been going off the rails recently and becoming quite a troublemaker. Tonight when he came home, he was different; he was nice. He has explained to me what had happened, and I didn't believe him, so he made me call you."

I explained what had happened that evening, confirming all that he had told her. She was amazed at what Jesus had done, and I arranged for us to meet with her and her son.

I got into bed and said aloud, "Yes, Lord, this is the real Christian life; thank you. I give you all the glory," and proceeded to go to sleep, marvelling on the wondrous things that God had been doing.

Later that night, I was woken from a deep sleep by a growling sound, which was getting louder and louder. As I came round and started to become aware of my surroundings, I expected the growling to stop because I thought I was dreaming it. However, as I sat up and rubbed my eyes, it continued to get louder. I sat up in bed and looked at the clock. It was about 1 a.m., and the growling was coming from everywhere. There was no direction; it just surrounded me like a stereo recording of some animal growling. It sounded like a vicious dog, but I sensed that this was the devil and his demons.

"Oh, it's only you," I said.

I was completely consumed by faith and security as I said this, and I laid back down to go back to sleep. As I pulled the quilt up over my torso, the growling suddenly stopped. I turned over and went back to sleep. This was another part of Matthew 8 that was about to open a whole new chapter in my life.

I would like to pause for a second and touch on what had happened on that glorious evening of outreach. There was one part of this testimony that I was unsure whether or not to include in this book. It was the part about taking authority over the rain. As I wrote this chapter, I prayed about it, and the Holy Spirit told me to include it because it is all part of the true testimony to God. The reason I was hesitant about including it was that I didn't want people to think that this was some weird unbiblical act. I mean, if I had read this in a book a few years ago, I would have thought the author was on drugs or something. If I had read it as an atheist, I would have challenged any Christian to do the same to prove it, knowing they couldn't and it wasn't true. As a dry, non-spirit-filled religious person, I would have dismissed it as an exaggeration and a coincidence.

Today, my view is that God can and does choose to do things like this through people. Does this mean that we can all go and command the weather to do what we want? Of course not; there would be complete chaos. However, God does choose to do things through us which might include, from time to time, taking authority over the weather and other natural elements. Moses parted the water, Peter walked on water, Elijah stopped the rain and said that none would come unless he commanded it to.

The most important part of all this testimony was that someone was saved and a life was changed for Jesus. It was a powerful example of how God wants us to co-labour with him. He had asked us to go out on this particular night. There were challenges and obstacles, but we had to be obedient every step of the way to see Jesus do what he wanted. We had to move our meeting. Then there was the rain; something had to be done about that because he had asked us to go out that night.

We attracted the young men because we appeared to be drunk, and they thought that was funny. The Holy Spirit took control of proceedings and overwhelmed two of us with the joy of his presence and uncontrollable laughter. The young men later said that they wouldn't have talked to us normally, but the laughter attracted them to us. In Acts 2, Pentecost came in such a noisy way that people thought the disciples were drunk and were attracted to what was going on (incidentally, this resulted in about three thousand being added to the church that day). On that night in our town, someone was saved, and through this powerful encounter, he fell on the ground, overcome by the presence of Jesus. He laid in the wet grass for a few minutes before getting up … not something anyone would want to do. All of this makes for interesting reading on how God works, all three persons of him: Father, Son, and Holy Ghost. It certainly opened my eyes as to how he works, and to top it all off, the devil, knowing that we had been co-labouring with God, tried to scare me off but was unable to. I now had a real sense that all of this was *very* real.

God really used this time to show me that the kingdom was indeed near, and this turned out to be a whole week of his testimony. All that week, he allowed me to see what it was like to be under a completely open heaven. Everything that I prayed for in the name of Jesus happened. Every sick person prayed for was healed by Jesus. Every non-Christian who was prayed over had an encounter with Jesus. This went on for the whole week, and then things went back to normal.

I again found that some people prayed for would be healed, and some people prayed for would not. I didn't understand why the Lord had shown me this open heaven for one week, but somehow, I knew that this was what we should all pursue. It was what he wants to see us doing. He is looking for a humble people who, out of love, will do his work. He wants us to be holy, set apart for him, righteous, and giving him all the glory. He wants a powerful, spirit-filled, and loving people to represent him. I would continue to pray for the sick and would continue to share the good news of salvation through Jesus Christ.

It is easy to become disheartened when we don't see those we have prayed for being healed. However, it is important that we continue to do the Lord's work regardless, purely because we love those around as and have compassion for them. I learned that I had to take my eyes off me, my performance, and without a care of how I looked, put them on others. To love others: This should be our motivation.

I was introduced to a gentleman, Jim, who had a terminal cancer, and I had been invited to go and pray for him. It was clear from my first meeting with him that he did not believe in Jesus, but in his utter desperation, he wanted to give prayer a try to see if he could be healed. I met with him on numerous occasions over a number of months and continually prayed for his healing. After the first few meetings, Jim commented on how the prayer seemed to ease his pain more than the painkillers, and every time we prayed, he could feel heat across where the cancer was. This opened up a conversation about Jesus, and I asked him if he wanted to accept Jesus as his Lord and Saviour. He agreed and prayed the prayer of repentance and accepted Jesus as his personal Lord and Saviour. What a glorious day that was, indeed.

I was convinced that the Lord was going to heal Jim of his cancer, and out of a desire to see him healed and his family restored, I continued to pray with him regularly. However, some time later, his condition worsened, and he died. It was great to know that he had accepted Jesus as his Lord and Saviour and now had taken his heavenly place, but I couldn't understand why he hadn't been healed. I took comfort in the knowledge that his salvation was the greatest miracle, even though I couldn't grasp why he hadn't been healed. It hurt to see the grief and pain of Jim's family, and in my compassion, I shared their pain over this loss. Mine was not the reason to know why; I knew God was good all the time and this had been a battle with the devil, which for some reason I had lost. Nevertheless, it hurt, having walked Jim's journey with him and his family.

At times like this, the devil tries to challenge your thinking and gets in your head: questioning whether you should be doing these things, getting you to examine if you are really doing God's will, questioning your identity as a child of God. My response was to read the Bible verses that the Lord had given me, to remind myself of all that God had done and to look for the next opportunity to serve him.

Some months later, we were spending the weekend at my in-laws' house. The time came for us to leave, and I packed the car for the journey home. Just as I was gathering my family and we were preparing to leave, the Holy Spirit told me to go and see Granny (Sarah's grandma), who lived in an annex attached to the house. I promptly went into the annex and sat down next to her. There was no one else in the room, and I wasn't sure why I was sat there because we were all ready to leave. I didn't have anything to say, so I just sat there.

Very soon after I sat down, Granny turned to me and asked, "Do you believe in life after death?"

"I do," I replied. "I believe that through Jesus, you can go to heaven for eternity."

She looked surprised and asked, "How do you know for sure? You seem very certain."

"I am certain, and the reason is because every morning when I wake up, I meet Jesus, who walks with me throughout the day. It never used to be like that, but it is different now because I asked him into my life, and I found out he is very real." I continued, "Do you know him like this?"

Granny replied, "No, I don't."

I asked, "Would you like to ask him into your life and also know that he is real and has a place in heaven for you?"

She replied, "Yes."

So I sat myself on the arm of her chair and rested my hand lightly on her shoulder. I led her in the prayer of repentance and accepting Jesus as her Lord and Saviour. As soon as we finished praying, I sensed Jesus walk into the room and approach her. All of a sudden, she looked at me, and her eyes widened, and she started to weep. I prayed for the Holy Spirit to come and fill her with his presence, and she started gasping for air as the fire of God hit her. Her face went red as the heat of his presence enveloped her more and more, and her gasping grew louder and louder.

Now, she was a very frail lady, and my prayers turned to thanking the Lord and then reminding myself that he knew what he was doing; I was getting concerned that he was going to take her to heaven there and then! After a while, she calmed down and started telling me about her encounter with Jesus that she had just experienced. We chatted for a while, and she revealed that she had two large lumps on her neck and was due to go to the doctors in two days' time. I prayed for her and commanded them to go in the name of Jesus. After this, I got up and left for my journey home.

Over the coming week, Granny called me to say that when she had gone to the doctors, her lumps had disappeared. It was a great miracle, but the greater news was hearing how she was constantly talking to Jesus each and every day. It was interesting to see what the Lord had done; she had been a regular attendee at a local church but had not really enjoyed an intimate relationship with Jesus. She was in a similar situation to me all those years ago, where the reality of God was nicely boxed in the corner of the room. She had been attending church but not encountering Jesus. Not having a real living relationship with Jesus meant that she was unsure if she would go to heaven. I had spent years in the same place as her in my dry, religious past, going to church but not encountering God. Fortunately, the Holy Spirit knew this and set up a divine appointment for us both that day.

Some months later, Granny died and went home to be with the Lord. I was honoured to attend her funeral, which was a mixture of grief for the loss of a beloved person and rejoicing in the knowledge that she was in heaven with her Lord and Saviour. As I talked to people at the funeral, it was obvious that she had shared with others her encounter with Jesus and subsequent relationship with him. Some of those people were Christians themselves, and they were overcome with joy at that funeral. It was a blessed time: grief and celebration and a testimony to the Lord. What a glorious thing it is that Jesus has done through the cross and his resurrection that we may be saved.

I am so glad that I never give up doing the Lord's work. It truly is a matter of life and death that we soldier on in the name of Jesus. There have been many occasions when prayers seem to go unanswered, when circumstances get difficult, but these are completely outweighed by the times when I see the Lord do something new. The Lord is gracious, and he has constantly sprinkled encouragement along the path to keep me moving in the direction he wanted. I really questioned myself about the validity of praying for the sick when Jim died. I felt that maybe I had misunderstood what God was saying and that maybe I shouldn't pray for the sick any more. It was time for the Lord to again renew my mind.

During that time of doubt, some visiting ministers from Nepal came to our church. They were used to undertaking God's work in an environment of extreme persecution and had seen many miracles. As we sat in the church, praying, the wife of one of the ministers came over to me and said she had a word from God for me. I listened in anticipation of the next words out of her mouth; she quoted Acts 10:38.

It was the verse God had shown me very early in this walk with him. God had now reminded me of that cornerstone passage and used this to encourage me to continue on. I am glad that I continued soldiering on for all those out there like Granny.

CHAPTER 12

An even crazier natural but still normal for the Lord

There had been many new experiences with the Lord which had really impacted both me and those around me. However, there was one surprising experience that I was not prepared for. It was the growling that I had heard in the bedroom that night. Even though I had dismissed it with the contempt it deserved, it brought home a reality of demonic activity that is often spoken about in the Bible but rarely taught in the church. In all those years of going to different churches, no one had ever really touched on the devil and demons. There had never been any teaching on how they operated and on how we as Christians have authority over them in the name of Jesus. This remained a part of Matthew 8 I had little experience of, but like everything else that had gone before, this was about to change. The Holy Spirit would take me through a new learning, both practically and in the Bible.

There was a large church not far from where we lived that was holding a series of meetings open to all churches. A small group of people from our church decided to attend, and I joined them for the four days of meetings. It was a well-attended event; even though the main hall of the church was large, there were a lot of people, and the church was quite full. People had come from many churches for this event.

As we took our seats at the first meeting, I was introduced to Jane, who knew someone in our party and had decided to come and sit with us. The meeting started with vibrant worship, which was led by a band, and people were encouraged to be free and worship how they felt they needed to. Some were dancing, some stood with their arms raised towards heaven, and some remained seated. The worship was great, going on for some time, and when it finally concluded, it was followed by the teaching of the word from the Bible. I found the teaching opened up fresh revelation, and also confirmed a lot of the Bible passages that the Lord had spoken to me.

At the end of the message, there was a call for prayer to receive healing. All those in the room who needed to be healed were invited to come forward for prayer. Jane stood up and moved to the front of the hall. As she went forward, the Holy Spirit said to me, "She won't be healed this time; there is more to this than meets the eye."

I was surprised at what I had heard and waited eagerly for her return. Sure enough, after being prayed for, Jane returned to her seat but was disappointed to report that she did not feel healed.

The next day, I sat with Jane over lunch. During the break, most of our group had remained in the church hall to eat instead of going outside. We moved the chairs around to create some space so that we could eat comfortably and chat. Most of the hall had emptied out, leaving behind a small number of groups dotted around the large hall, eating and talking.

SIMON BETHEL

As Jane and I chatted away, I learned that she had been suffering from severe back pain for a number of years. The pain was affecting her job as a nurse, restricting what she could do to help others. She was also a very active Christian and part of a vibrant evangelical church in town. As we continued to talk, I shared a little of my story and some of the things that I had seen God doing recently, especially regarding healing.

"Would you pray for my back?" she asked.

"Yes," I replied.

I was very conscious of what the Holy Spirit had said to me the day before. I wasn't sure what he had meant, but I prayed regardless.

We stood up, and she closed her eyes. I placed my hand in the middle of her back and started to pray, "I command healing into this back in the name of Jesus."

As I prayed, I was taken aback by a dramatic change in her face. All of a sudden, during the prayer, her face contorted and screwed up into a very strange shape. The best way I can describe it was that it looked like one of those old statues of a Chinese dragon. Her face took on a definite shape similar to this. She then dropped to her knees and started to lean back. She went further and further back until she was at an angle of about 25 degrees to the floor. All the time this was happening, I had kept my hand in the middle of her back. I was not entirely holding her up; she seemed to be levitating. As she lowered towards the floor, I knelt down beside her, and because of the position I was in, my face was very near to hers. I suddenly found myself staring at this very strange appearance, face to face. Being so close, I felt a presence of complete evil in that face before me. It was so powerful, and I was shocked at the physical feeling of such an evil presence. I was now in completely new territory; this was beyond anything else I had come across in my life. I didn't know what to do, so I asked the Holy Spirit.

He replied, "Command it to get out and leave."

"I command you to leave in the name of Jesus," I said firmly and with authority. "Come out of her in the name of Jesus."

As I said these words, she started screaming. It was a very loud scream, and at first, it startled me. I continued to pray. The screaming increased in intensity and started to echo around the large room, drawing the attention of everybody who was having lunch. In fact, it was so loud that the church leaders heard it from the other side of the church building. They came running in to see what was happening. As they burst through the doors, Jane let out a sigh and then slumped to the floor on her back. I prayed for the Holy Spirit to fill her in the name of Jesus, and she remained there on the floor for about two hours.

During this time, everyone returned to the hall, and the meeting resumed. There was more worship, more teaching, and more prayer. Jane just stayed there on the floor motionless, and from time to time, members of our group would check on her and pray over her.

As the meeting progressed, she slowly got up off the floor and sat on her chair. I was keen to find out what had happened but had to wait until the end of the meeting before I could speak to her again.

"What happened when we prayed earlier?" I asked.

She answered, "When you prayed, I felt my face contort. It was uncontrollable, and I couldn't seem to do anything about it. I am not sure what it was doing. I just felt that it had done something strange. As you continued to pray, it felt like something was being dragged out of me. Whatever it was, it didn't want to leave, and it felt like claws were scraping up the inside of my body, trying to hang on. When it was finally dragged all the way out, I felt exhausted and like a weight had been lifted. I was then filled with a feeling of peace and freedom. As I lay on the floor, I encountered the Lord Jesus."

"How is your back now?" I asked.

"It still hurts," she replied.

"Let's pray for it again," I said, "but shall we do it tomorrow? You have been through a lot today."

"Yes, that makes sense," she replied. "I feel quite drained. Let's do it tomorrow."

The next day, we all reconvened together for the next meeting at the church. As people gathered for the meeting, I prayed for Jane's back again. As before, I placed my hand in the middle of her back and said, "I command healing into this back in the name of Jesus."

Instantly, she fell on the floor. This time, there was no commotion like before; she simply fell on the floor. The church meeting began. We had worship, and a word was given from the Bible. Jane remained on the floor for about three hours. When she finally got up, she was pleased that there was no pain in her back; the Lord had done it again. Thank you, Jesus.

This had been a real revelation, something that I had never come across before. First, there had been the growling, and now this. I was now acutely aware of demons at work. This was new to me, and I relied upon the Holy Spirit and my reading of the Bible to understand better where and how the demons were involved in situations. This was one topic that those around me really struggled to understand; some were in complete denial that demons were real and active.

It is interesting that when you read the Bible, there are a lot of references to healing and deliverance. These are very difficult subjects for people to accept in modern-day Western society. In years gone by, I too would have dismissed these concepts as irrelevant, but I was now left with no doubt that it was very real.

When Christians would challenge me on this subject, one of the ways that I would try to open their thinking would be to ask this question: "Jesus delivered people from evil spirits. He told others to deliver people from evil spirits. As a Christian, do you believe that Jesus knew what he was talking about?"

All Christians would reply, "Yes."

I would then continue, "Well, you either believe what Jesus said or you don't. If you don't believe what he said, then you are effectively calling him a liar. Which one is it?"

My sole purpose in saying this was to bring people to believe that everything Jesus said was true and that all the things he talked about and taught still apply today. We have simply lost sight of this reality. All those years I had gone to church, I had blinkers on and never saw the full truth or understood the breadth of spiritual activity. To be a Christian is, by its very definition, to be spiritual. To be filled with the Holy Spirit is spiritual; the spiritual realm is real, and this was a truth I had missed for all those years as a Christian who had boxed God up in the corner.

I never appreciated the reality of the spiritual realm. I never understood the part it played, and I had never received any teaching. There are many people today who go to church with the same perspective that I used to have. I used to be a dry Christian, not spiritual, and had certainly not received the Holy Spirit. However, I had now received him, and it was through his knowledge and power that I was being led through situations like the one with Jane. We need to understand the importance of having this spiritual discernment. To have discernment, we need to have the Holy Spirit... God's spirit in us; it is that simple. 1 Corinthians 2:10–14:

> These are the things God has revealed to us by his Spirit.
>
> The Spirit searches all things, even the deep things of God. For who knows a person's thoughts except their

own spirit within them? In the same way no one knows the thoughts of God except the Spirit of God. What we have received is not the spirit of the world, but the Spirit who is from God, so that we may understand what God has freely given us. This is what we speak, not in words taught us by human wisdom but in words taught by the Spirit, explaining spiritual realities with Spirit-taught words.[c] The person without the Spirit does not accept the things that come from the Spirit of God but considers them foolishness, and cannot understand them because they are discerned only through the Spirit.

In the New Testament, people had to be full of the Holy Spirit to have knowledge and discernment for the most menial of tasks (Acts 6). If it was a prerequisite to be filled with the Holy Spirit in order to undertake a menial task, then how much more is he needed for doing greater tasks for the Lord? In Acts 6, the apostles were looking for someone to wait on tables and feed the widows. This was a task that they felt needed to be handed to some other disciples so that they could focus on praying and teaching. They needed to choose someone, but there was a prerequisite: to be filled with the Holy Spirit in order to serve on tables. I mean, surely serving food is a small task in the church and doesn't require much training? However, even to just do this, they had to be people filled with the Holy Spirit. Acts 6:1–6:

> In those days when the number of disciples was increasing, the Hellenistic Jews[a] among them complained against the Hebraic Jews because their widows were being overlooked in the daily distribution of food. So the Twelve gathered all the disciples together and said, "It would not be right for us to neglect the ministry of the

word of God in order to wait on tables. Brothers and sisters, choose seven men from among you who are known to be full of the Spirit and wisdom. We will turn this responsibility over to them and will give our attention to prayer and the ministry of the word."

This proposal pleased the whole group. They chose Stephen, a man full of faith and of the Holy Spirit; also Philip, Procorus, Nicanor, Timon, Parmenas, and Nicolas from Antioch, a convert to Judaism. They presented these men to the apostles, who prayed and laid their hands on them.

Surely, the same applies today? To undertake the most menial of tasks today in the body of Christ means that we should be filled with the Holy Spirit. Being filled with the Holy Spirit then brings about spiritual discernment when undertaking the Lord's work. If we are not filled with the Holy Spirit then we are doing things in our own strength and are less effective for God. Again, I learned the truth of this in a practical way.

One day, a group of us had been on the streets to spread the good news of Jesus. We finished our outreach and returned back to church and cleaned everything away. As we prepared to leave for home, one of the women in the group asked for prayer. Ellie explained that she had a problem with her stomach. She had not been able to eat properly for nearly two years; every time she had eaten a good hearty meal, she had been ill. Over this period, she had been forced to eat small meals and many different foods to try and keep it in her stomach. The doctors had been unable to identify the problem, despite extensive tests. She had also received prayer on a number of occasions from numerous people since the problem had first started, but despite this, it had persisted.

We all gathered round and laid hands on Ellie. As people started to pray, I asked the Holy Spirit to reveal what the cause of the problem was. He showed me a picture of a serpent that was wrapped round her stomach. It was a spirit of infirmity.

I started to pray, "I command the spirit of infirmity to leave in the name of Jesus. I cast out the serpent spirit wrapped around the stomach and command you to leave in the name of Jesus."

As we continued to pray, one of the other people praying looked at me wide-eyed and said, "Wow, I had a picture of a snake come into my mind a few moments ago, and I couldn't understand why. Now I understand why, and I know that you saw it too."

This was confirmation of what the Holy Spirit had shown me. So we continued to pray, and as we did, Ellie shook as we commanded the spirit of infirmity to leave. After a while, she stopped shaking, so we stopped praying. From that day onwards, she was able to eat freely, and the symptoms disappeared completely. It was another example to me of the spiritual realm; this time, I was encouraged to hear someone else see the same things that I saw. The person who had seen the picture of a serpent was a recently saved Christian and so quite new in her faith. She was hearing from the Holy Spirit and experiencing the things of the spiritual realm so early in her walk with the Lord. It was exciting to see this happening.

This type of event became a regular occurrence. I was not only asked to pray for healing, but it seemed that deliverance went hand in hand with all that was asked of me. On another occasion, I received a phone call, asking for prayer for a man who couldn't sleep. Wesley, a lady from the church, and myself agreed to go and pray over them.

OH MY GOSH! .....IT'S ALL REAL!

As arranged, we arrived at his house and sat down to listen to Brian explain the situation to us.

Brian started, "I can't sleep at night because I have terrible nightmares that wake me up. I keep having to sit up and am constantly hallucinating. This is happening every night, and I end up in cold sweats. They are horrible. It's really tormenting me."

"We will go around the house and pray," I said, "and anoint the door frames with oil, if that's okay. I've had the Lord speak to me, telling me to read Psalm 91 to you." And I read out the psalm.

Now, I know that this is a popular psalm, but I had never read it before. The Holy Spirit told me to read it out loud, so I had obeyed. As soon as I had completed reading Psalm 91, the lady from church asked Brian, "Do you understand that God loves you? As the Psalm says, he is there for you. Do you know Jesus?"

"No," he replied.

"Would you like to know him?" she asked.

"Yes," he answered.

She led him in a prayer of repentance and asked Jesus into his life. Hallelujah, Brian was saved. We then went around to the bedroom and prayed, casting out all spirits and anointing the door frames with oil. We prayed over the bed and then all around the house, commanding every evil spirit to leave in the name of Jesus.

Now, if you had bumped in to me many years ago and told me that you had done this exact same thing, I would have thought you were missing a few brain cells. I wouldn't have thought this was a sensible thing to do. But here I was, doing that exact thing because now, I was fully aware of the spiritual realm and the reality of what goes on. How wrong I had been in the past. What was the outcome of the prayer? From that night onwards, Brian slept soundly every night. Not a nightmare or cold sweat in sight.

Anointing the door frames with oil and casting out evil spirits from the house was a new experience for me. It was great to see Brian set free and come to faith. I was on a real learning curve, being led by the Holy Spirit's teaching. I was starting to look for spiritual explanations for the things that happened around me. Whereas previously, I would have understood and dealt with situations with my natural mindset, I was now discerning the spiritual aspects of those situations through the Holy Spirit.

One particular day, it was my friend's birthday. A lot of people found it difficult to get along with this friend. He was argumentative, not very forgiving, and very judgemental of others. He would say whatever he wanted, even if it offended someone. I had bought a present and card for him and was going to drop it round. I telephoned him to wish him happy birthday, but he shouted at me on the phone and said he didn't want the card or present. He was very rude.

My daughter, Alex, overheard the conversation and was shocked with what had happened. In the past, I would have put the phone down and not bothered with him anymore, but now I had spiritual discernment that made me an overcomer, so I could shine the light of Jesus.

I explained to Alex, "God has shown me that this particular individual has two demons that are wreaking havoc in their lives. On this occasion, he slammed the phone down on me."

"What are you going to do?" she asked.

As she asked, the Holy Spirit gave me the solution: "We are both going to pray over this birthday card and anoint it with oil," I replied. "It will just be like Paul and the handkerchiefs in Acts 19."

So Alex and I prayed over the birthday card and anointed it with oil. We then went and slipped it through my friend's letterbox. We arrived back home to the telephone ringing. It was my friend, who called up to apologise and invite us round for some food. My daughter again saw the power of prayer at work in a dark situation.

Acts 19:1–12:

> While Apollos was at Corinth, Simon took the road through the interior and arrived at Ephesus. There he found some disciples and asked them, "Did you receive the Holy Spirit when[a] you believed?"
>
> They answered, "No, we have not even heard that there is a Holy Spirit."
>
> So Paul asked, "Then what baptism did you receive?"
>
> "John's baptism," they replied.
>
> Paul said, "John's baptism was a baptism of repentance. He told the people to believe in the one coming after him, that is, in Jesus." On hearing this, they were baptized in the name of the Lord Jesus. When Paul placed his hands on them, the Holy Spirit came on them, and they spoke in tongues[b] and prophesied. There were about twelve men in all.
>
> Paul entered the synagogue and spoke boldly there for three months, arguing persuasively about the kingdom of God. But some of them became obstinate; they refused to believe and publicly maligned the Way. So Paul left them. He took the disciples with him and had discussions daily in the lecture hall of Tyrannus. This went on for two years, so

that all the Jews and Greeks who lived in the province of Asia heard the word of the Lord.

God did extraordinary miracles through Paul, so that even handkerchiefs and aprons that had touched him were taken to the sick, and their illnesses were cured and the evil spirits left them.

I had certainly had my eyes well and truly opened to the truth now. Jesus had been filled with the Holy Spirit at his baptism to do all the things that he needed to do. He had told others to be filled with the Holy Spirit and said that they would do the same things that he had been doing – and they did. Today, it is exactly the same. Nothing has changed. God is the same yesterday, today, and tomorrow. We need to be filled with the Holy Spirit to do the same things Jesus did. I had now experienced all of Matthew 8: healing, deliverance, the calming of the weather. It is all true and applies just as much to the world today.

CHAPTER 13

Worship? Really?

It was 2008: the year the world was hit by a financial crisis. Banks had to be bailed out, and stocks and shares crashed. For various reasons, like many, I was hit very hard financially; 2008 would prove to be a very tough year. As the first part of the year progressed, it became increasingly difficult to keep the finances from sinking deeper into a hole. Each month became a battle for survival. I was getting anxious about what to do, as I couldn't see how to resolve the situation; we ran out of money so early in the month.

In my increasing anxiety, I took the situation to the Lord. One evening, I walked into the bedroom, closed the door, and knelt on the floor. I asked God for guidance and for his help because I wasn't sure how to climb out of the hole I seemed to be in. I was shocked and surprised at the immediacy of his response. I was also surprised at what he said.

As I knelt there, I heard the Lord say, "Worship."

"Worship?" I responded in surprise. "I don't feel like worshipping. I am desperate and need help, and I don't feel like worshipping."

"Worship," was his answer.

I continued to pray, trying to turn my prayers requesting help into worship. I found it difficult because I was overwhelmed with the circumstances around me. I was gripped by fear and anxiety as to what the future held. In desperation, I put on some worship music to help and started to sing. After a while, my attention turned to the Lord and not my circumstances. I was starting to lose the feeling of oppression and despair, which was now being replaced with hope and faith.

Over the coming weeks, I continued to worship. Each time I did, I could feel his presence and comfort consuming me. During the next few months, God started to intervene in my finances and brought about numerous miracles that changed the outlook of my financial position. His provision was both practical (quickly selling a car to aid my cash flow) and supernatural: One morning, I came down the stairs. Everyone was in bed, and I was the first person up. As I walked down stairs, there in the hallway was a pile of £20 notes, just sitting there.

This was not the first or the last supernatural intervention in our finances. Very quickly, circumstances changed from running out of money early in the month to having just enough money to see us through the whole month. Within five months, God had brought about radical changes to my financial position.

This was a surprising revelation to me of how I should continually worship and exalt him at every opportunity. I learned that heartfelt worship was not just only reserved for church services; it was for everywhere and anytime. As I reflected on what had happened, I was reminded of the story of Jericho in the Bible; a similar thing had happened in my finances. Through my shouts of praise and adoration to the Lord, the walls of my financial situation had crumbled, and God had delivered a victory. It was a very strange way to approach the battle, but it was God's way..... I still had much to learn. Previously, I had sung worship songs at church and in the car, but until then, I'd never taken time at home just to worship him. I had come to understand that as well as the need to make time to pray at home, I also needed to carve out time for worship. I found that my heart for worship grew. I would put on worship songs at home and sing out praise, with my very being to exalt him. Then, one day, God spoke to me as I worshipped and asked me to set up a fellowship meeting. I was to create an environment for free worship, a place with no boundaries, where he had the freedom to do what he wanted. I agreed.

I spoke to Wesley and also to my very close friend, Sue, about what God had asked me to do. We agreed to meet one evening a fortnight to worship God. We had no band and no structure; we just had a heart for God and the desire to worship him and be close to him. We used one of the rooms at church for our meetings; the first gatherings consisted of me and Sue putting on worship DVDs and singing and dancing before God. Each time we met, we praised and worshipped the Father and Son and invited the Holy Spirit to lead us.

As we sang and danced, the presence of God would fall on us, and we would enjoy being intimate with him. Some nights, we would laugh and shout with joy; other nights, we would be on the floor face down in humility before the Lord. It wasn't long before more people joined us at these meetings. We had an open invitation for anyone to come and be closer to God, and we maintained the same approach of having no agenda and allowing God to do what he wanted. We had no finish time, just a start time and a hunger to worship and encounter God.

As the months progressed, we were joined by a guitarist, and the worship moved from following DVDs to live music, and the whole meeting was led by the Holy Spirit. Over time, more and more people started to come to the meetings from other churches. I was never hung up on how many people came; we averaged about twenty people, so it was nothing too big. I was more concerned with people having an encounter with their Father and being filled with the Holy Spirit.

With a few more people in attendance, we started to see the Holy Spirit doing different things. One week, we would sing and worship for an hour and a half, and then everyone would be on the ground, prostrate before the Lord. Another week, there would be less worship, a word given, and ministry (prayer). Sometimes, the Lord would give me a word to speak prior to the meeting; other times, he would give me a word during the worship, or he would tell me someone else had a word, and I was to give space for them to speak. It was great seeing how the Holy Spirit worked when given the freedom.

One of the biggest learning curves for me at these meetings was seeing the different ways in which people reacted when they encountered God's presence. Some wept, some laughed uncontrollably, and some fell to the floor; there were lots of different reactions. On more than one occasion, people foamed at the mouth in the heavy presence of God, and we would pray for deliverance from demons.

In the early meetings, I found all of these manifestations uncomfortable; this was new territory for me, and I had to be sensitive to the Holy Spirit to understand what was happening. I needed to be sure that with everything that happened, we honoured God and each other. I relied on the teaching of the Holy Spirit and evidence in the Bible to reaffirm that everything was of God. During this time, I learned to work with the Holy Spirit closely. I needed to because it was him who was at work and not me.

One particular day, a young woman came to the meeting. We had enjoyed an extended time of worship, and once the singing and dancing concluded, we shared a word about someone in difficulty, to which she responded. She came forward for prayer, and as I prayed over her, she started to speak in tongues. Now, I would never normally interrupt someone doing that, but the Holy Spirit said, "She needs to stop striving and just wait on God."

So I broke in and said, "Sorry to interrupt, but the Holy Spirit is saying to be still, not say anything, and wait on God."

She was silent for a few minutes and then started speaking in tongues again.

"She needs to stop striving and wait on God," the Holy Spirit repeated.

"Shhh, just wait on God," I said, and she stopped again.

Moments later, I felt a wind come up from behind me and rush past me, ruffling my hair as it did. The wind blew past me and hit the woman, who was standing in front of me. As the wind blew on her face, her hair was blown back, and her eyes widened as she stared at me. Then all of a sudden, she started to weep uncontrollably. She wept and wept for what seemed to be an age. She wept so much that her top got quite wet from all the tears. I had never seen anyone cry so much as this. After weeping for some time, she fell on the floor and stayed there for about three hours. The Holy Spirit showed me that she was having an encounter with the Lord and that she was being comforted over difficult situations. Personally, I was still amazed at the manifest presence of the wind and what God had been doing. It had taken me completely by surprise.

On another occasion, a woman who had previously been healed by the Lord brought a man on crutches to the meeting. He had fallen off some scaffolding and broken the bones in both his feet. He wasn't a Christian and had only ever been to church to attend a few weddings and funerals. We began the meeting as usual, and by the end of worship, he appeared to be a little agitated. I asked if he was okay.

He explained, "As we sang, during one of the songs, the room disappeared before my eyes, and I saw a vision of a church on fire. It was on fire but not being consumed by flames. Then, a little later, as we sang, I saw a number of angels around the room. They were worshipping with us."

He was overwhelmed by it all.

We discussed the vision for a while, and I put him at ease with all that had been happening. Then, when it came time for ministry, we prayed for him to be healed. As soon as we finished praying, his feet started to make funny clicking sounds. We were all amazed at the noises that were coming from his feet; after a short while, he reported that the pain had left, and he started to walk around the room without his crutches. This clearly made an impact on him, so we led him in a prayer of repentance and accepting Jesus as his Lord and Saviour. As we prayed, he started to get hot, as the presence of the Lord descended on him. Later, he said it had been so hot, it was like someone had poured a fire over him. At the end of the meeting, he left with his crutches under his arms, walking unaided out of the building. As he walked away, we praised the Lord for all he had done, giving him all glory.

While we packed everything away, someone came up to me and remarked, "Praise the Lord! It is great to see what he does. That chap who came tonight as an unbeliever has experienced more in one night than I have in all my years of attending church. I will surely press in for more of God's presence."

Another evening, we were setting up for a meeting, getting the chairs out, the guitar rigged up, and so on.

OH MY GOSH! .....IT'S ALL REAL!

One of our regular attendees, Sue, rushed through the door and exclaimed, "I've just come from hospital. My son is there, and he's really poorly; they told me they can't do anything and to prepare for the worst. As I sat there in the hospital, I just knew I had to come to our meeting and refuse to accept what has been said."

"We will pray for him and stand with you in refusing to accept this," I replied.

As we worshipped, the Lord reminded me of a Bible verse and that I should speak it out as we finished our worship. Once we had finished singing, we started to pray and I read out Luke 7:11–15:

> Soon afterward, Jesus went to a town called Nain, and his disciples and a large crowd went along with him. As he approached the town gate, a dead person was being carried out—the only son of his mother, and she was a widow. And a large crowd from the town was with her. When the Lord saw her, his heart went out to her and he said, "Don't cry."
>
> Then he went up and touched the bier they were carrying him on, and the bearers stood still. He said, "Young man, I say to you, get up!" The dead man sat up and began to talk, and Jesus gave him back to his mother.

Now, Sue was herself a widow, so we started to claim this healing for her son. It was about 9:15 p.m., and one of the other women in the meeting tapped her watch and said, "He will start to get better from now."

After much prayer and calling on God, we closed the meeting. The next day, Sue went to visit her son and found that he was sitting up in bed, his temperature had returned to normal, and he was taken off the oxygen mask. A couple of days later, she contacted me and said there had been a complete turnaround in her son's health, and he was due to be leaving hospital. It was such a change from being told to prepare for the worst. It transpired that he had started to improve the moment we had prayed; at 9.15 p.m., Jesus had raised him up.

Sue later explained to me that she had been in this situation before, and previously, she had called people to come down to the hospital to pray over her son. However, this time, when she had been told all was lost, her natural instinct was to stay with her son, but she felt God telling her to come to the meeting. She felt that she just had to be there to pray with us.

I was now in a place where I had truly seen God's grace and real response to prayer, fasting, and worship. I was completely in awe of all that God was doing. During the day, I had a job which people envied; it was exciting, rewarding, and I often received a number of enquiries as to how to get into a career doing the same work. Now, with all that God was doing, my exciting day job seemed boring in comparison.

God impressed on me that he wanted to do more; this was exciting. I felt that we needed to go to prayer and increase in our hunger for God. Wesley and I agreed that we should have a twenty-four-hour continuous prayer event at our local church, where we would cry out to God for revival. There was a small room adjacent to the main church hall, and we decided to open it up for twenty-four hours of continuous prayer. We compiled a rota of people who would begin praying on a Saturday morning, continuing all the way through to Sunday morning. This meant that we would finish praying at the same time the church service started. Wesley and I agreed between us that where there were empty slots that were not taken by others, we would fill them ourselves to ensure there was a continuous twenty-four hours of prayer.

Prayer began Saturday morning and continued throughout the day. I did a couple of evening slots and was then due to go back for a slot in the early hours, three to five o'clock in the morning.

When I arrived back into the room at 3 a.m., I was met by Wesley, who had been praying and worshipping. We continued to pray and cry out to God together. As we prayed, the atmosphere began to change. The air started to get heavier, and it felt like gravity itself was increasing. Before I knew it, I was on the floor, laying on my back, next to Wesley, who was also pinned to the floor.

As I lay there, I was aware of God's presence just in front of my face. It was as if the whole of heaven was laid open, centimetres away from me. The atmosphere was thick, heavy, and glorious. I had never felt anything like this before. We both stayed on the floor, unable to get up, basking in the glorious presence of the Lord. It was quite some time before I could find the strength in my legs to get up and return home. We lived a five-minute walk from the church, and I praised God all the way home for meeting us in that room. As I climbed into bed and my head hit the pillow, I prayed that there would be a similar encounter when I returned before the church service in a few hours. I had an expectation and a hunger.

Sunday morning, I arrived back at church an hour before the service was due to start. As I walked across the hall towards the small room, I could feel the same manifest presence of God. It increased as I walked nearer, and when I entered the room, I rejoiced that the Lord's presence was still there. I stayed in that room until it was time for the church service to start. As I walked back into the church hall, I was surprised and pleased to hear people commenting on the presence that they could feel.

One person remarked to me, "I can't believe it; it's beautiful. The presence is just oozing out of the room and into the church hall. It is like a slow-running river running from that room. I love it."

Many people were taken by surprise at God's tangible presence; they had never experienced anything like it before. I never wanted his presence to stop, and I knew that we would have to continue to pray and be hungry to see more of his lasting presence.

Unfortunately, the church was not set up to allow continual prayer. During most days, the church hall was hired out to various groups, and therefore, it was not possible for us to continue with twenty-four hours of prayer. Without prayer and with a lack of hunger, this tangible presence of God lifted. A few of us had learned that we needed to be desperate for God and on our knees, praying, to see more of his presence. However, there were insufficient numbers of people to be able to influence the church to go after God in total abandonment. Not everyone was hungry and desperate to seek God in worship and truth. 2 Chronicles 5:11–14:

> The priests then withdrew from the Holy Place. All the priests who were there had consecrated themselves, regardless of their divisions. All the Levites who were musicians—Asaph, Heman, Jeduthun and their sons and relatives—stood on the east side of the altar, dressed in fine linen and playing cymbals, harps and lyres. They were accompanied by 120 priests sounding trumpets. The trumpeters and musicians joined in unison to give praise and thanks to the Lord. Accompanied by trumpets, cymbals and other instruments, the singers raised their voices in praise to the Lord and sang:

"He is good;
 his love endures forever."

Then the temple of the Lord was filled with the cloud, and the priests could not perform their service because of the cloud, for the glory of the Lord filled the temple of God.

CHAPTER 14

Conclusion

How amazing is the grace of God? A wonderful life changing experience has been testified to in this book. I cannot comprehend the size of his love. The Father's love is evident by him sending his Son to die for all of us so our sins would be forgiven. The love of Jesus is evident in the price he paid for us through his death and resurrection and also through his continued love for us. The Holy Spirit is evident and real in all that he has done; prior to the last few years, he was the missing part of God in my life.

As he has done for countless others, God has been gracious all the way through my journey from a hard-hearted atheist who denied God's very existence, through my years as a dry religious churchgoer, to a spirit-filled Christian in a very real relationship with the Holy Spirit. Throughout my journey, I have made many mistakes and taken many detours from God's path, as I have traversed the landscape of the natural world, but through the blood of Jesus, God has been forgiving and gracious. There is hope for everyone and enough grace to forgive all who truly repent. I have not been to theology college, nor am I an ordained minister. I am simply a man off the street with a hunger and passion to follow Jesus. My passion is for everyone to know the truth, the truth about pursuing the rawness of God, who constantly colours outside the lines; there is no boxing him up in the corner. I have learned the truth about his desire to have an intimate relationship with us. It is for all, regardless of your background.

God has shown so much to a simple man off the street; I have listed in sections below my conclusions of the most important things I have learned

All of it is real.

First and foremost, he showed me that it is all real and relevant today. God the Father, God the Son, and God the Holy Spirit: all real. The Bible is true, and the acts of God it speaks about are true. He is still doing the same things in this generation. Like myself, countless others have experienced these very real and living acts in their lives today. I was so wrong in my atheist thinking. All the events in this book are true; there is no possible way that I could have conceived to make all these things happen and then actually bring them to reality. Only God could do that.

Know Him Intimately

Reflecting on my journey so far, I can testify that God's love, grace, and mercy are so big that it is incomprehensible to the human brain. Any unworthiness I felt in the past is now history. To have made so many mistakes and to have wandered so far off God's path and yet be completely forgiven and loved through the blood of Jesus Christ is amazing. I have come to learn that God is love, and he loves me dearly. I am compelled to love him back with all that I am. It is not a decision; I have an overwhelming feeling of love for him. I no longer feel lonely but am constantly warmed by the true feeling of his love and acceptance (and I mean physically warmed by his presence). Everywhere I go, I am aware of his presence; he sees me as spotless because of what Jesus has done for me. My life so far has been an adventure of two parts. In part one, I was trying to choose my own path in my own strength, firstly as an atheist and then as a dry religious churchgoer. I didn't comprehend there was a guide who could walk intimately with me and lead me in the right direction. Knowing him would have made the journey much more enjoyable. Now, in part two, I know he is actively involved, choosing a much better path for me. I just had to find him and get to know him, and thankfully, now I do. He is my father, my daddy; he is God Almighty. Romans 8:

> For those who are led by the Spirit of God are the children of God. The Spirit you received does not make you slaves, so that you live in fear again; rather, the Spirit you received brought about your adoption to sonship. And by him we cry, "*Abba*, Father." The Spirit himself testifies with our spirit that we are God's children. Now if we are children, then we are heirs—heirs of God and co-heirs with Christ, if indeed we share in his sufferings in order that we may also share in his glory.

As a child of God, I am a co-heir with Jesus and a representative of God. He not only wants us to be his representatives, he also wants us to represent Jesus to others so that they too can have a relationship with him and the Father. Only if we *know* him intimately and have a real relationship with him can we represent him to others. To know someone well, you have to spend time with them, talking and listening, interacting with them. Only then, when you have a true two-way relationship, will you really *know* them. It is the same with

Jesus: You need to know him. The old saying goes like this: "You know when you know that you know because you know that you know." The Holy Spirit helps move that knowing from your mind to your heart and every part of your being. Ephesians 1:15–17:

> For this reason, ever since I heard about your faith in the Lord Jesus and your love for all God's people, I have not stopped giving thanks for you, remembering you in my prayers. I keep asking that the God of our Lord Jesus Christ, the glorious Father, may give you the Spirit[f] of wisdom and revelation, so that you may know him better.

Receive the Baptism of the Holy Spirit

The baptism of the Holy Spirit is a normal part of the Christian life. It is for everyone. Not receiving the Holy Spirit is like missing a part of God. I struggled with this at first. In all my years of going to church, the baptism of the Holy Spirit hadn't been taught, and because of this, the dry religion in me found it a difficult thing to grasp. Others who also didn't understand would often say to me that it wasn't necessary and felt that they were being made to feel like second-class Christians for not being filled with the Holy Spirit. There are no first- or second-class Christians, only spirit-filled Christians. Over time, God revealed to me that this was a "must do" by showing how Jesus needed this baptism to undertake his ministry. In the New Testament, it was reaffirmed many times that believers needed to receive the Holy Spirit. God promised us the Holy Spirit because we also need the same baptism.

In Western society, we have been conditioned to be logical in our thinking and have generally grown cynical of spiritual things. Through this hardness of heart, we have found it difficult to receive the Holy Spirit. By its very definition, to receive something, you need to be ready to accept it first, and this is where a lot of people falter … me included, all those years ago. It is healthy to test things but also important not to dismiss the fullness of God, like I did for so long. I have learned that God is not a pick-and-choose buffet, where you can select the parts of him that you want and then ignore the other parts you are uncomfortable with. He offers a full menu for us, and only when we have eaten everything are we truly satisfied. I did it for years, just selecting part of the menu and then wondering why I wasn't satisfied; many people still do this today. They select the parts they are comfortable with and then question why they are not fully satisfied. For years, I missed out the part of the menu that was the Holy Spirit. It is the power of the Holy Spirit and this anointing that teaches us and empowers us to co-labour in God's strength and not our own. The Holy Spirit is a real, practical companion who lives in us; we need to let him take his place. He permeates God through every part of our very being. Without him, it is in our mind and not in our very being. All those years before my baptism in the Spirit, I went to church knowing about God, knowing about Jesus on the cross, but I didn't *know* him.….. I didn't have compelling arguments, and my faith could be shaken. As soon as I was baptised in the Holy Spirit, I began received his teaching. I felt his very real presence. I began to know him and was unwavering in my faith. But first I had to be ready to receive him and ask for our baptism. In Luke 11:11–12, Jesus says:

> "Which of you fathers, if your son asks for a fish, will give him a snake instead? Or if he asks for an egg, will give him a scorpion? If you then, though you are evil, know how to give good gifts to your children, how much more will your Father in heaven give the Holy Spirit to those who ask him!"

This baptism is for everyone, not a select few...it's for you, for me, everyone. In Acts 2, Peter talked about the Spirit being poured out on all people. Acts 2:14–18:

> Then Peter stood up with the Eleven, raised his voice and addressed the crowd: "Fellow Jews and all of you who live in Jerusalem, let me explain this to you; listen carefully to what I say. These people are not drunk, as you suppose. It's only nine in the morning! No, this is what was spoken by the prophet Joel:
>
> "'In the last days, God says,
>   I will pour out my Spirit on all people.
> Your sons and daughters will prophesy,
>   your young men will see visions,
>   your old men will dream dreams.
> Even on my servants, both men and women,
>   I will pour out my Spirit in those days,
>   and they will prophesy.'"

This baptism of the Holy Spirit is just a natural part of being a Christian. Acts 8:14–17:

> When the apostles in Jerusalem heard that Samaria had accepted the word of God, they sent Peter and John to Samaria. When they arrived, they prayed for the new believers there that they might receive the Holy Spirit, because the Holy Spirit had not yet come on any of them; they had simply been baptized in the name of the Lord Jesus. Then Peter and John placed their hands on them, and they received the Holy Spirit.

To quote this verse in Acts 8: have you simply been baptised in the name of Jesus and not had the Holy Spirit come on you? Have you received the Holy Spirit? Have you had your Pentecost?

Be Humble and Allow Yourself to be Lead

These pages are about someone moving from an arrogant, boastful, and uncaring atheist to someone who became humble before God, about taking his eyes off himself and looking at others in love and compassion, being humble with a desire to honour God and those around me. It has been a story of encounter with the Lord and the power of the spirit. I found the secret to accessing all the things of God, and it is this: to be in his presence. I have learned a phrase of how to position myself for the things of God: "lower and slower." The lower on the ground and the more time we spend with him, the more humble we will be. When people look at me, I want to be so low that they look straight past me and see Jesus, not Simon. If they see me, then I have simply got in the way. We need to consecrate ourselves to God and be holy and righteous in our living, constantly spending time with God every day. There is a simplicity to just being in his presence and interacting with him, which we need to grasp hold of. There are too many distractions and complications in life today.... we need to grasp the simplicity of just being with God. Once we have been with him, and he has revealed his will, we can move forwards from that position. In my early years of undertaking youth work in the church, I relied mostly on books and planning a structure to everything. After being baptised in the Holy Spirit, I can see how I did so much of it in my own strength and without God. This changed after I received the Holy Spirit. I was led by him.

OH MY GOSH! .....IT'S ALL REAL!

One Sunday morning, I was leading the youth Sunday school. I prayed the day before to ask the Lord what he wanted to do, and he responded by showing me an activity he wanted me to do with them. It was something I had heard years before; it focussed on the fact that as Christians, we are children of God. God being our Daddy, Abba, and Father. I recognised that the activity would only take up half of the time allocated for Sunday school and was unsure what would happen for the second half, but the Lord was clear that I should do that activity only. On Sunday morning, there were about thirteen youth in the class. As planned, we went through the activity together, and as we concluded, I recognised the presence of the God in the room.

Suddenly, the demeanour of the youth started to change. As his presence increased and the air got heavy, most of them started crying; of the remainder, some started laughing, and others just sat quietly. I sat down and prayed, just leaving the Holy Spirit to do what he was doing and not getting in his way. The second part of the meeting was left for him to run, and he did a deep work in people, I remained in my seat while he continued. This approach to Sunday school was a stark contrast to the shallow slick presentations and games I used to play with them in the days before the Holy Spirit changed me.

Being baptised in the Holy Spirit brought a new approach to everything I did, in and out of church. There was still planning, but now I stopped first and spent time with God to understand what he wanted to do and how he wanted to do it. I then planned from that starting position, always giving him space to change things. By spending time with him, I could put his plans in place. I also found that often, he didn't want a plan; he wanted me to just follow the Holy Spirit into situations and be led: no plan, just listen and obey the Holy Spirit.

Don't Be Distracted; Be with Him

Initially, I found it hard to just stop everything and be with him; there were simply too many distractions. I started at first by doing a little worship and praise, followed by just resting and talking with him. It took a while to get into the habit, but eventually, after continually taking the time to seek him, I started to find that his presence would arrive quicker each time I sat down to pray.

It is important that we find that Upper Room with God, shutting out the distractions. This is a very important point, and I can't emphasise it enough. Remember when Jesus took me from lounge to lounge, with all those people ignoring him while they watched TV? We need to find a way to shut out the distractions and spend time in his presence because he desperately desires to spend time with us. Two of the biggest distractions today are the Internet and social media. It is easy to become addicted to them. Just like alcohol, drugs, or sex: The Internet can also become an addiction that takes us away from God's presence. We need to be very mindful of the things that can steal our time away from God. I read recently that the average churchgoer spends about seven minutes a day in prayer. God desires to spend time with us, and he wants more than seven minutes.

As I spent time with God, I learned that the feeling of his presence was more powerful and exciting than anything else that I could possibly experience in the natural. Sometimes, I felt like I had been plugged into an electrical mains socket, as wave after wave of electricity permeated through my body. Other times, it was so hot that I felt like I was in front of a fire, and yet other times, the air was so heavy, I couldn't stand. These were all feelings that happened when I was in the presence of God. One time, I had been spending time with God in my study when someone from church called round. I invited them in, and as they walked past my study, they fell to the floor from the power of the presence of God. James 4:5–8:

Or do you think Scripture says without reason that he jealously longs for the spirit he has caused to dwell in us? But he gives us more grace. That is why Scripture says:

"God opposes the proud
 but shows favour to the humble."
Submit yourselves, then, to God. Resist the devil, and he will flee from you. Come near to God and he will come near to you.

Discern Spiritual Activity

Another lesson was about the reality of the devil and the demonic: the role they play in illness, oppression, and possession. As I researched healing and deliverance in the Bible, I was surprised by how many times they are mentioned. Before receiving the Holy Spirit, I had heard little teaching on this subject, but he showed me that as children of God, through the blood of Jesus, we have authority over demons and illness.

Ephesians 6:10–12:

> Finally, be strong in the Lord and in his mighty power. Put on the full armour of God, so that you can take your stand against the devil's schemes. For our struggle is not against flesh and blood, but against the rulers, against the authorities, against the powers of this dark world and against the spiritual forces of evil in the heavenly realms.

1 John 4:1–4:

> Dear friends, do not believe every spirit, but test the spirits to see whether they are from God, because many false

> prophets have gone out into the world. This is how you can recognize the Spirit of God: Every spirit that acknowledges that Jesus Christ has come in the flesh is from God, but every spirit that does not acknowledge Jesus is not from God. This is the spirit of the antichrist, which you have heard is coming and even now is already in the world.
>
> You, dear children, are from God and have overcome them, because the one who is in you is greater than the one who is in the world.

We are to use our authority as Christians to spread the light and undo the darkness. Jesus came to spend time with the sinners so he could share the good news and heal the sick. He constantly coloured outside the lines. Today, he expects us to go out to the sinners and spread the good news; he expects us to heal the sick, and he expects us to colour outside the lines too. We are to advance the kingdom of God and undo the works of the devil just like Jesus did … and still does today. We are not destined to sit, pray, and take no action. In my journey, God made it clear that he wants to use us.

Have a More Powerful Testimony for the Next Generation

As a father and a husband, it has been really important that I soldier on against persecution so that those around me are unable to deny the truth and reality of the whole Christian life. Bearing fruit, giving testimony, and bringing tangible evidence of God at work has been instrumental in deepening the faith of those around me and convincing them to pursue a deeper relationship with Jesus. When God has spoken things to you and they have come true, when God has revealed things that you couldn't know and you speak them out, when people have been healed of illnesses where there is no known medical cure, and when the reality of demons has been exposed, then it is inevitable that those around you will also come to know the truth because they see what has been happening.

All of my children have seen the Lord heal people, and this has in turn deepened their own faith. One of my sons prayed for a man who had suffered for twelve years with an issue with his nerves. He had been taking constant medication to ease the symptoms throughout those twelve years. Thomas prayed for him at the front of a youth gathering, and the Lord instantly healed him. It is safe to say this had a big impact on Thomas in strengthening his faith.

We live in a modern day of animation where computer-generated images in movies and computer games easily distract our children into wonderful worlds of make-believe and fantasy. These distractions help them create clear boundaries in their minds between the events of the natural world and those that are saved exclusively for a world of fantasy. This results in a belief that supernatural and spiritual things are not real but are things saved for make-believe, alongside such fictitious beings as zombies. We are in a battle for our children's minds, and we need to know what is going to win them over.

The answer to this for me has been a living testimony of all that God has done in my life; this has redrawn the line in a different position for my children. By encouraging them to heal the sick and experience the reality of Jesus, they have been firmly planted into the truth of everything that God does today. Their boundaries on what is real have shifted, giving them a clear perspective on what is authentic and what is fiction. They see the greater reward and experience in adventures with God than in the world of fiction.

A few months ago, I walked into the lounge, where my kids were watching TV. They were watching a science fiction programme about someone battling aliens. As I walked past, the scene on the TV cut across to a gargoyle-like figure.

I looked at it and commented, "Yes, I have come across a few things that look like that in my time. In the real world, guns don't deal with them; you need the authority of Jesus to deal with them. That is greater than any gun. I know you enjoy watching this, but it is much more of an adventure in the real world."

They all smiled because they knew what I meant and agreed.

As parents and Christians, we have a responsibility to lead by example so that our children know the truth of what makes up a full Christian life. They need to see a Christian life that includes testimony of co-labouring with the Lord and testimony of the things we have seen him do, a Christian life of interaction and intimacy with God, a spirit-filled life. God is looking for a generation who are spirit filled and on fire for Jesus. A generation that is snatched out of the devil's hands and taken into a deep relationship with Jesus. A generation who will walk in the fullness of what it means to be a Christian, not entering dark places to be consumed by darkness but shining the light of Jesus so that others come to the light. We all have a part to play in leading our kids to the truth. My children have told me how they have shared the testimony of the things they have seen with non-Christians. These testimonies have opened up a whole new dimension to their witness of Jesus and broken down barriers where people would have been hard of heart.

I want to close with a few verses from Psalm 78.

The first few verses speak about how we need to constantly be reminded of what God has done and then to spread his testimony from generation to generation.

In verses 8 and 9, there is a stark warning against being hard of heart and forgetting the testimony of what God has done; we need to remind ourselves of all that God has done, to remain expectant that as we co-labour with him, he will do more.

In verse 9, we read about the men of Ephraim, who stood on the battlefield, ready to fight, but then forgot all God had done. In verse 11, they walked off the battlefield, even though they were dressed ready to fight; we need to be ready to fight in the full knowledge of who we are in Jesus, not to forget or to dilute all he has said and who we are. The moment we choose to dismiss what he has said and believe that it is not *all* real and refuse to accept all that God has for us, we have started to walk off the battlefield.

Despite all of this, in verse 23, even though the people broke God's covenant, he still performed miracles and gave them new testimony; we need to understand that it is God's nature to be there for his people and to do miraculous things. The testimony about what God has done is powerful and needs to be at the forefront of our minds. Our own powerful testimony needs to be shared from generation to generation. God does not stop giving us testimony.

In verses 19–20, they forgot the miracles he had performed, and so in disbelief, they questioned God's ability to do things for them in the present; doesn't that sound familiar? It is similar to a lot of the thinking today, that God doesn't do miracles anymore or that we don't see them; his very nature is brought into question.

Yet in the following verses, he did the miracles they asked for; guess what? He still does miracles today. I think there are some very poignant points in this verse for us today:

Psalm 78

A maskil of Asaph.

My people, hear my teaching;
  listen to the words of my mouth.
I will open my mouth with a parable;

SIMON BETHEL

I will utter hidden things, things from of old—
things we have heard and known,
  things our ancestors have told us.
We will not hide them from their descendants;
  we will tell the next generation
the praiseworthy deeds of the Lord,
  his power, and the wonders he has done.
He decreed statutes for Jacob
  and established the law in Israel,
which he commanded our ancestors
  to teach their children,
so the next generation would know them,
  even the children yet to be born,
  and they in turn would tell their children.
Then they would put their trust in God
  and would not forget his deeds
  but would keep his commands.
They would not be like their ancestors—
  a stubborn and rebellious generation,
whose hearts were not loyal to God,
  whose spirits were not faithful to him.

The men of Ephraim, though armed with bows,
  turned back on the day of battle;
they did not keep God's covenant
  and refused to live by his law.
They forgot what he had done,
  the wonders he had shown them.
He did miracles in the sight of their ancestors
  in the land of Egypt, in the region of Zoan.
He divided the sea and led them through;

OH MY GOSH! .....IT'S ALL REAL!

he made the water stand up like a wall.
He guided them with the cloud by day
  and with light from the fire all night.
He split the rocks in the wilderness
  and gave them water as abundant as the seas;
he brought streams out of a rocky crag
  and made water flow down like rivers.

But they continued to sin against him,
  rebelling in the wilderness against the Most High.
They willfully put God to the test
  by demanding the food they craved.
They spoke against God;
  they said, "Can God really
  spread a table in the wilderness?
True, he struck the rock,
  and water gushed out,
  streams flowed abundantly,
but can he also give us bread?
  Can he supply meat for his people?"
When the Lord heard them, he was furious;
  his fire broke out against Jacob,
  and his wrath rose against Israel,
for they did not believe in God
  or trust in his deliverance.
Yet he gave a command to the skies above
  and opened the doors of the heavens;
he rained down manna for the people to eat,
  he gave them the grain of heaven.
Human beings ate the bread of angels;
  he sent them all the food they could eat.

> He let loose the east wind from the heavens
>   and by his power made the south wind blow.
> He rained meat down on them like dust,
>   birds like sand on the seashore.
> He made them come down inside their camp,
>   all around their tents.
> They ate till they were gorged—
>   he had given them what they craved.
> But before they turned from what they craved,
>   even while the food was still in their mouths,
> God's anger rose against them;
>   he put to death the sturdiest among them,
>   cutting down the young men of Israel.
>
> In spite of all this, they kept on sinning;
>   in spite of his wonders, they did not believe

So in closing, I have a question and a challenge:

The Question

First and foremost, do you know it is all true? Have you accepted the Lord Jesus as your Lord and Saviour? Do you know you are headed for heaven? Have you received the Holy Spirit? If not and you would like to embark on a new exciting life with Jesus, then please pray the prayer on the next page.

The Challenge

Now, my challenge is this: Regardless of what you do for a living, your background, where you live……. what testimony are you going to give people? How are you going to set an example to your kids, your family, your friends? What testimony to Jesus will you be? Will it be a testimony to the truth of living the full Christian life? There will be a definite day that will come in your life, and it is this: On the day you close your eyes on this earth for the very last time and you then open them in heaven, will you leave behind a testimony to the Lord and be able to stand before God and show him all you have done for him?

Prayer for salvation

God, I know that, in my lifetime, I have not always lived for you, and I have sinned in ways I probably don't even know yet are sins. I know that you have plans for me, and I want to live in those plans. I pray to you for forgiveness for the ways in which I have sinned.

I am choosing now to accept you, Jesus, into my heart. I now accept you and declare you as my Lord and Saviour. I am eternally grateful for your sacrifice on the cross and how you died so I can have eternal life. I pray that I will be filled with the Holy Spirit and that I continue to live as you desire for me to live. I will strive to overcome temptations and no longer let sin control me. I put myself – my life and my future – in your hands. I pray that you work in my life and guide my steps so that I continue to live for you for the rest of this life.

Amen

Printed in Great Britain
by Amazon